stock

market

timing

made easy

and EXACT

THE 7 WAVE Heccis Cycle

HECTOR CISNEROS

Order this book online at www.trafford.com
or email orders@trafford.com

Most Trafford titles are also available at major online book retailers.

Printed in the United States of America.

ISBN: 978-1-4120-5731-8 (sc)
ISBN: 978-1-4907-5096-5 (e)

Trafford rev. 11/06/2014

www.trafford.com

North America & international
toll-free: 1 888 232 4444 (USA & Canada)
fax: 812 355 4082

CONTENTS

CHARTS

Dedicated to the memory of

Ralph Nelson Elliott

whose formidable

creation of the wave principles,

inspired my discovery of

the Heccis Cycle

INTRODUCTION

Cycles, in financial bar charts have been my investigative passion for 25 years. To my knowledge, there has never been a theory, system or method, to exhibit a cycle, *exactly*. Working with orderly ascending and descending bars, called waves, I wanted to improve confusing cycle theories, that implies a cycle, but lacks verifiable evidence of starts to completion theory. A cycle is defined as, *an interval of time during which a sequence of recurring successions of events or phenomena is COMPLETE*. It seemed reasonable to me, if this succession of wave events could be proofed out to a completion, and it precisely recurs again and again, I would be on track. It was my dream as well as other chartists, to find or discover a system, that could pick stocks at their lowest or highest point, CONSISTANTLY and EXACTLY. Gradually with an introduction of pivot points (A) and (B), I saw a trust-worthy discovery beyond my dreams. It's a formula (not a theory) of locating eight elusive pivot points, which accurately pinpoints market reversals. Counting each bar between these specifically numbered pivot point, ends a complete seven-wave cycle of bars, and begins the next cycle trend to the opposite bull or bear direction. This perpetual phenomena of 7 cycles reversal, appears in all bar charts and time frames, delivering constant entries and exits, EXACTLY …. beyond your wildest dreams.

A simple mathematical formula that I call the "Heccis Cycle", transforms an ordinary looking bar chart into a decision making instrument that investors can master with ease, and use with confidence. The best-suited charts to easily understand the formula are the quarterly and monthly, and with experience you can learn as well to develop the weekly and daily Time Frame charts.

Observe the exact timing of entries and exits as the seven waves of the Heccis Cycle develops. It's written with an intended minimum of words… enough to be understood, without confusing and superfluous information. The accompanying 43 chart studies of stocks, commodities and indicies should be carefully observed and compared. It illustrates many examples that serve as information that words alone cannot describe.

It may seem complicated at first glance, but it's really simple. Select your charts…follow the rules…and I promise, you will be constantly amazed as I still am, when you easily validate at pp(C). With practice you will say…"I got it!"

WHAT IS
THE HECCIS CYCLE?

1. A MECHANICAL BAR CHART COUNTING METHOD THAT EXACTLY IDENTIFIES BEGINNINGS AND ENDINGS OF MARKET CYCLES.

2. IT EXACTLY IDENTIFIES EIGHT SPECIFIC CYCLE REVERSAL BARS, CALLED PIVOT POINT BAR (pp), FOR BETTER MARKET ENTRIES OR EXITS.

3. A SET OF ACCOMPANYING ZIG-ZAGGING BARS, CALLED "WAVES"
   BEGINS WITH A NUMBERED pp BAR, AND ENDS AT THE NEXT NUMBERED pp BAR.

   EACH WAVE REVERSES ITS UP OR DOWN TRENDING DIRECTION, AFTER EACH pp BAR.

4. IT'S APPLICABLE TO ALL FINANCIAL BAR CHARTS.

5. IT'S APPLICABLE TO ALL TIME FRAME BAR CHARTS, FROM MINUTES TO YEARLY.

6. ALL RULES AND THE FOUR PRINCIPLES ARE APPLIED EXACTLY FOR UP (BULL) … AND, DOWN (BEAR) MARKET CYCLES.

DEFINITIONS

1. **BARCHART**

Each perpendicular bar represents a measure of time and the price range it covers in its respective Time Frame

2. **FINANCIAL MARKETS**

The Heccis Cycle applies to all bar charts, (Stocks, commodities, futures, mutual funds, indices, etc.) and in all Time Frames.

3. **TIME FRAMES**

Each chart will indicate its time frame.
YEARLY………… one bar = 1 year
QUARTERLY…. one bar = 3 months
MONTHLY……… one bar = 1 month
WEEKLY……….. one bar = 5 days
And so on to include days, hours, minutes.

4. **CYCLE …for the Heccis Cycle method**

Each time frame has its own MAJOR cycle consisting of eight specific pp bars and seven waves. Between each of the eight pp's a MINOR cycle or an a,b,c, may occur with its own eight pp's and seven waves which cannot be distinguished in long term time frames, such as quarterly and monthly charts.
Major or Minor cycle ending at ppC, starts a new cycle, trending up or down to the opposite direction.

5. **WAVES**

One wave contains a series of zigzag bars trending in one direction, from one pp to the next pp.

EXPLANATION

IDENTIFYING THE SPECIFIC
8 PIVOT POINTS IN THE HECCIS CYCLE
EMPLOYS TWO METHODS

VISUAL WAVES
AND
BAR COUNTING

Method No.1
VISUAL WAVES
SHOWN AS DASH LINE WAVES
Fig.1 and Fig.2

VISUALLY, THE HIGHEST BAR pp (C),
STARTS A BEAR MARKET TREND,
…..AND THEN SEEKS THE NEXT LOWEST BAR
pp2., WHICH IN FIG. 1, IT'S THE SAME
LONG BAR AS pp(C)
…AND THEN

- THE VISUAL DASH LINE CONTINUES TO THE NEXT HIGHEST BAR pp3
- THEN TO THE NEXT LOWEST BAR pp4…
- THEN TO THE NEXT HIGHEST BAR pp5…
- THEN TO THE NEXT LOWEST BAR ppA…
- THEN TO THE NEXT HIGHEST BAR ppB…
- THEN TO THE NEXT LOWEST BAR pp(C) THE END OF THIS CYCLE IN ANY TIME FRAME.

EXPLANATION

Method No. 2

BAR COUNTING

ARCHED LINES WITH NUMERALS
Fig.1 and Fig.2
INDICATE THE TOTAL NUMBER OF
BARS COUNTED

Example Fig. 1 Explained….
AFTER APPLYING THE VISUAL DASH LINE, THE NUMBER OF BARS ARE COUNTED FROM pp2 TO pp5…THE ANSWER (6 BARS …IN THE ARCHED LINE), INDICATES THAT 6 OR (100%) MORE BARS WILL FOLLOW TO END THE COMPLETE CYCLE FROM pp5 TO pp(C.)

TO DETERMINE THAT pp(C) IS A VALID CYCLE ENDING BAR, ANOTHER BAR COUNT IS MADE FROM pp4 TO ppB…. THE ANSWER …(5 BARS…. IN THE ARCHED LINE), INDICATES THAT 3 OR (60%) MORE BARS WILL FOLLOW TO END THE COMPLETE CYCLE FROM ppB TO pp(C.)

WHEN BOTH THE 100% AND THE 60% COUNTS TERMINATE ON THE SAME pp(C) BAR,
THE COMPLETE EIGHT PIVOT POINT CYCLE CONCLUSION HAS BEEN CONFIRMED, FROM pp(C) TO pp(C).

Example Fig. 2…follow above instructions.
See Cycle Rules…page 16

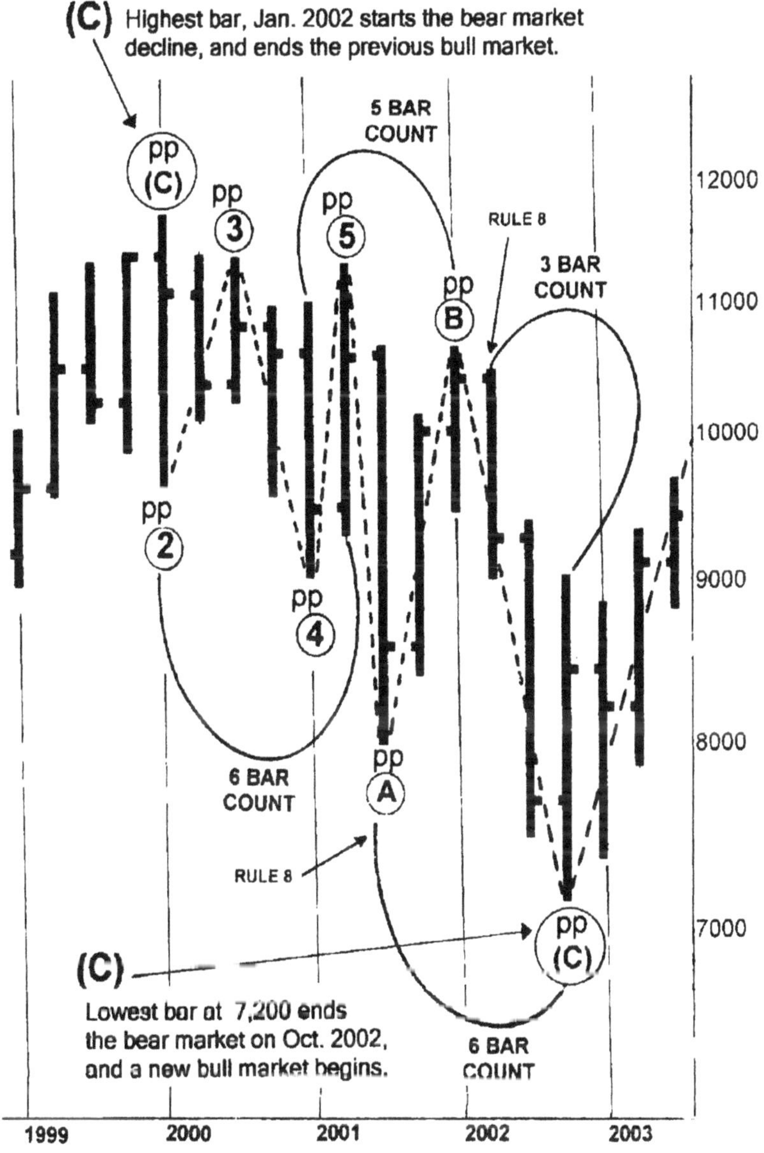

EXAMPLE FIGURE 1

DOW JONES INDUSTRIAL

MONTHLY

1 Bar = 1 Month

The eight pps from pp(C) to pp(C) are placed on this Monthly chart as it appears on the Quarterly chart (Fig .1).
Then the four principles and rules are applied, to indicate the precise Monthly pp bars.

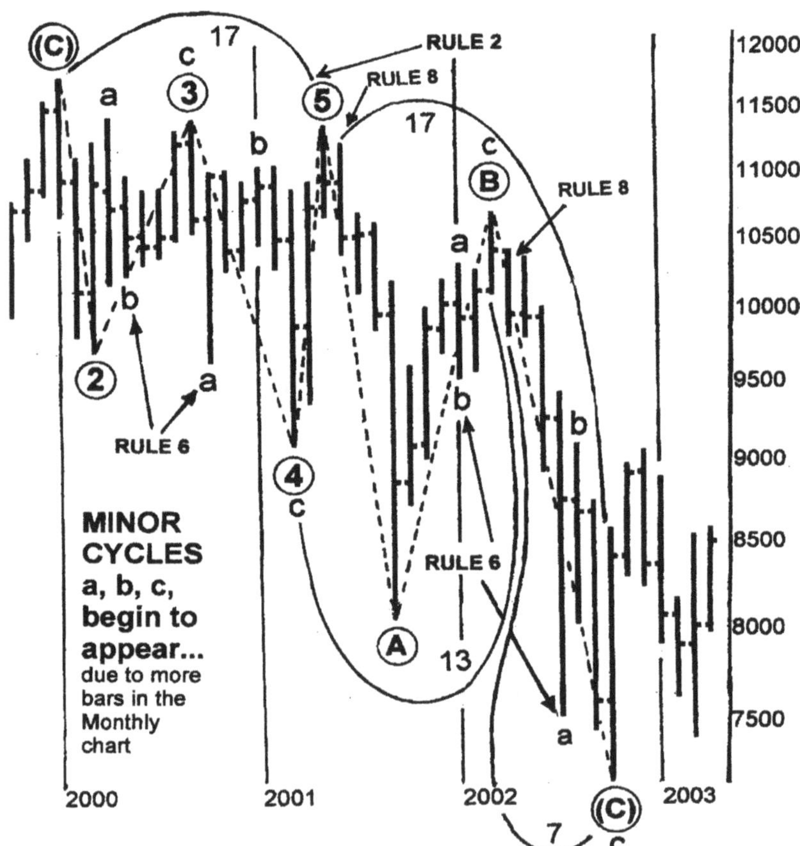

EXAMPLE FIGURE 2

THE FOUR PRINCIPALS OF THE HECCIS CYCLE

APPEAR IN ALL BAR CHARTS
AND IN ALL TIME FRAMES
(Illustrated in Fig.1 ang Fig.2)

1. 8 PIVOT POINT (pp) REVERSALS
pp(C)...pp2...pp3...pp4...pp5...ppA...ppB...pp(C)

2. VISUAL SEVEN WAVES...
completes a cycle from pp (C) to...pp (C)
A BEAR MARKET begins when the highest bar, pp (C) starts a series of down trending zigzag bars to the lowest pp(C) bar is reached at bottom.

A BULL MARKET begins when the lowest bar pp(C) starts a series of up trending zigzag bars to the highest pp(C) bar is reached at the top.

3. BAR COUNT ADDITIONS FROM pp2 TO pp5
The total bars from pp2 to pp5 are added up... then 60% or 100% of this addition, will result in the number of bars from pp5 to pp(C)...the end of a complete cycle.

4. BAR COUNT ADDITIONS FROM pp4 TO ppB
The total bars from pp4 to ppB are added up...
Then 60% or 100% of that addition will result in the number of bars from ppB to pp(C)...the end of a complete cycle

CONFIRMATION

The ending bar, pp(C), that results from the addition of pp2 to pp5 and the same bar pp(C), that results from the addition of pp4 to ppB ...will confirm the cycle conclusion.

ABOVE FOUR PRINCIPLES AND ALL RULES APPLY EXACTLY, FOR BULL AND BEAR MARKET CYCLES

THE TEN RULES OF THE HECCIS CYCLE

1. Always count bars from pp(2) to pp(5) to determine the number of bars from pp(5) to pp(C)

2. If pp(2) to pp(5) does not result in a good verified count to attain a valid pp(C) – try pp(C) to pp(5)

3. Always count from pp(4) to pp(B) to determine the number of bars from pp(B) to pp(C).

4. In all charts the bar counting **FROM** pp(5) **OR** pp(B) can either be 100% or 60% to reach pp(C).

5. To determine the 60% of a number, use the first digit only. Example: 60% of 13 bars, equals 7 bars, not 7.8 and do not round out to 8.

6. MINOR CYCLES…or an a, b, c, is formed, as more bars appear, due to a Time Frame of more bars

7. When two or more bars are horizontally aligned, any ONE of those bars can be valid for a pp bar count.

8. At any pp(5) or pp(B), the bar counts can start on same pp bar or the following bar.

9. An adjacent bar can become valid to have a proper count.

10. Different Time Frames of the same stock, are permitted to locate their pps on other bars, as long as the 4 Principals is maintained.

    Note:(When Rule Numbers appears in charts, the above stated rule has been applied to that chart.)

CONSTRUCTING THE HECCIS CYCLE ON A CHART

Investors can choose the best Time Frame Charts suited for their style of trading. It is best to begin with a Quarterly or Monthly chart, because the Four Principles can be easily applied on these shortened charts with fewer bars. The next 2 pages illustrate the progress of one Time Frame to the next.

Transfer the eight pp positions of the Quarterly or Monthly chart, to the same pp location on a Weekly Time Frame chart. And again apply the 4 Principles.

Some charts require a slight shift of bar location to accommodate a valid bar count. See Rule10. Do not attempt the Daily transfers until totally familiar with the Weekly charts.

The seven-wave cycle principle presents an investing opportunity at each of its eight pp bars. Knowing that each of it's seven waves terminate at a specific pp bar, and then reverses it's trend to the opposite direction and towards the next pp bar, the investor can determine the market trend for entering or exiting a position. Remember, all Time Frames have the Heccis Cycle. For example the bars on a monthly chart as Phelps Dodge on page 34 can appear as a weekly or a daily Time Frame in another chart.

Although all charts shown are past history, with knowledge of the Heccis mechanics it can be managed and bar counted as the waves develop in real time, from each of its 8 pp bars, in all Time Frame charts.

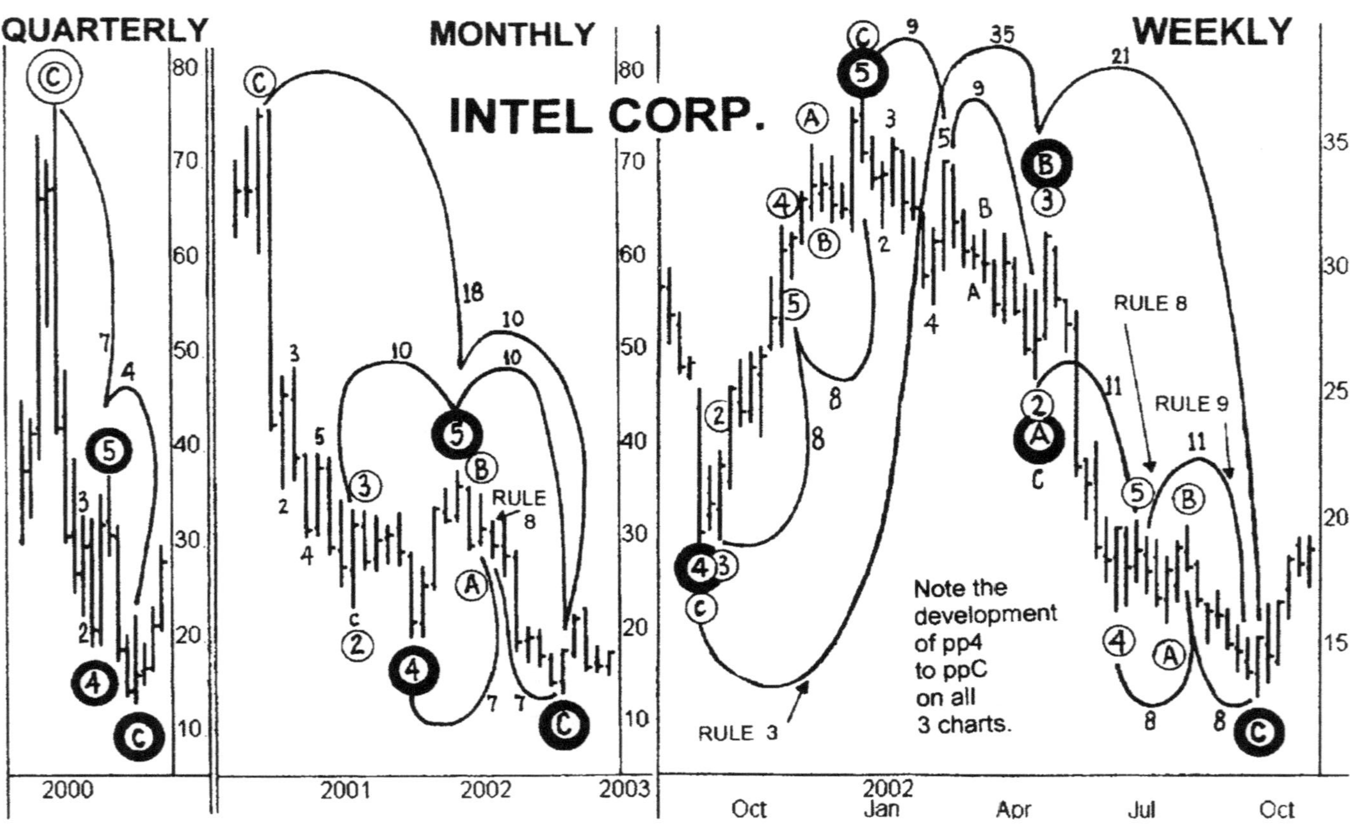
INTEL CORP.
QUARTERLY
MONTHLY
WEEKLY
RULE 3
RULE 8
RULE 9
Note the development of pp4 to ppC on all 3 charts.
2000
2001
2002
2003
Oct
2002 Jan
Apr
Jul
Oct

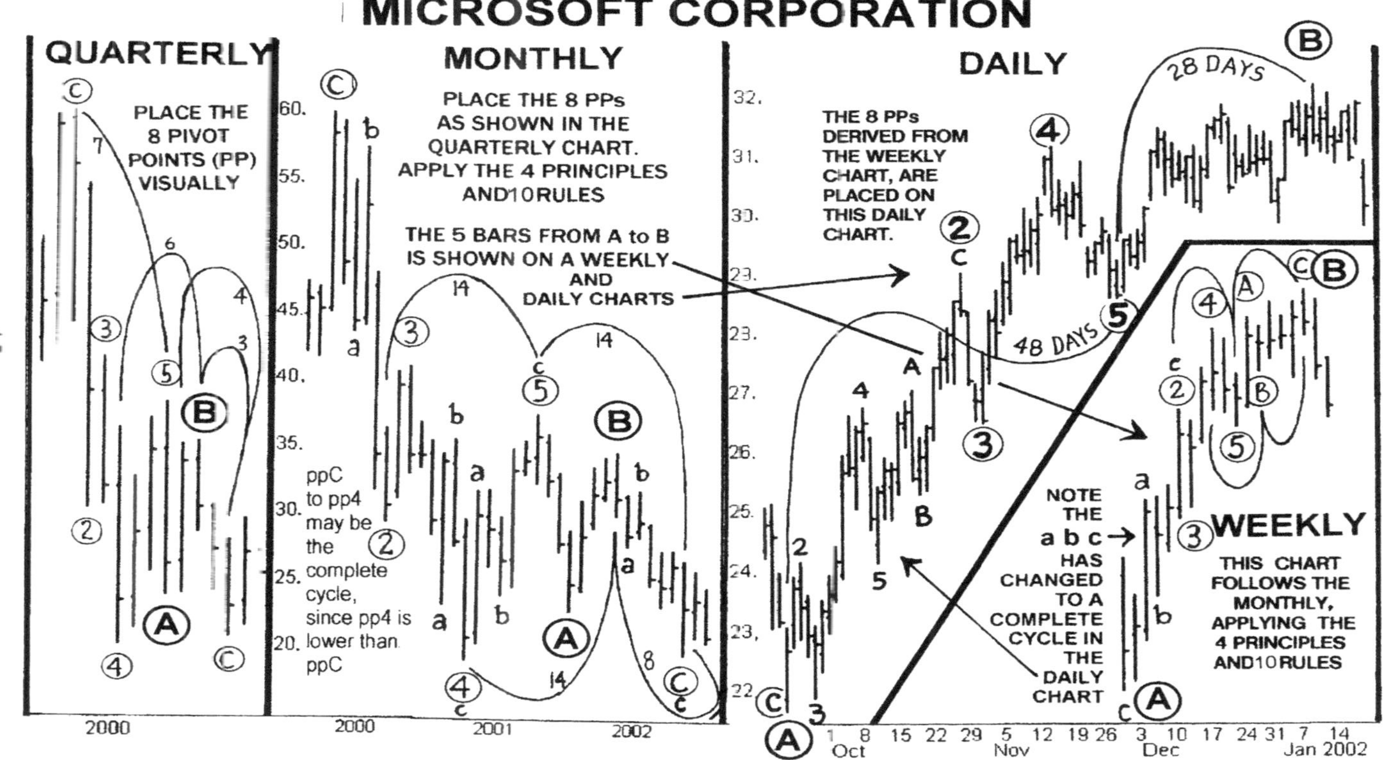

CYCLE FORMATIONS FROM ccA TO ccB...on different Time Frames
MICROSOFT CORPORATION
QUARTERLY
PLACE THE 8 PIVOT POINTS (PP) VISUALLY
MONTHLY
PLACE THE 8 PPs AS SHOWN IN THE QUARTERLY CHART. APPLY THE 4 PRINCIPLES AND10RULES
THE 5 BARS FROM A to B IS SHOWN ON A WEEKLY AND DAILY CHARTS
ppC to pp4 may be the complete cycle, since pp4 is lower than ppC
DAILY
THE 8 PPs DERIVED FROM THE WEEKLY CHART, ARE PLACED ON THIS DAILY CHART.
28 DAYS
48 DAYS
NOTE THE a b c → HAS CHANGED TO A COMPLETE CYCLE IN THE DAILY CHART
WEEKLY
THIS CHART FOLLOWS THE MONTHLY, APPLYING THE 4 PRINCIPLES AND10RULES
2000
2001
2002
1 8 15 22 29 5 12 19 26 3 10 17 24 31 7 14
Oct
Nov
Dec
Jan 2002

A PICTURE IS WORTH A THOUSAND WORDS

The following charts, illustrates the formula of the seven wave Heccis Cycle in action, clearly attesting to the merits of this tool for technical analysis. A careful study of each chart is worth more to you than a page of words. It's in this analysis that you can learn and familiarize yourself with different aspects of this exact counting formula.

After you have gained knowledge, attempt the exercise on your selected charts, perhaps following thru to weekly and daily charts. If questions arise, the answers are probably in the 10 Rules, the Four Principles, or the 2 Explanation sections.

Very few charts do not fulfill exactly the Heccis Cycle rules, but none have I found to be at random. Some disguise their pp's in extraordinary fashions, making it difficult and time consuming to apply the 4 Disciplines of the Heccis Cycle. Extended, contracted, or corrupt bars and other data errors, will affect the chart structure for bar counting purposes. If you find the Heccis formula not working, try another Time Frame or better, select another chart. Be aware that market swings are unpredictable. Approach all pivot points as strong possibilities of reversals, and act only when it actually reverses.

Like most chartists, when their dream is fulfilled, they claim no system better than theirs. My method is a stand-alone system with the user possibly not having any knowledge of technical analysis. No need for indicators, patterns, channels, news, trends, or fundamental analysis, not to mention, behavioral analysis. If you practice the Heccis Cycle you will rightfully conclude, that "everything is in the charts!" Even most fundamentalists will join ranks with ease and declare this phenomena, "a scientific event" that constantly delivers market direction.

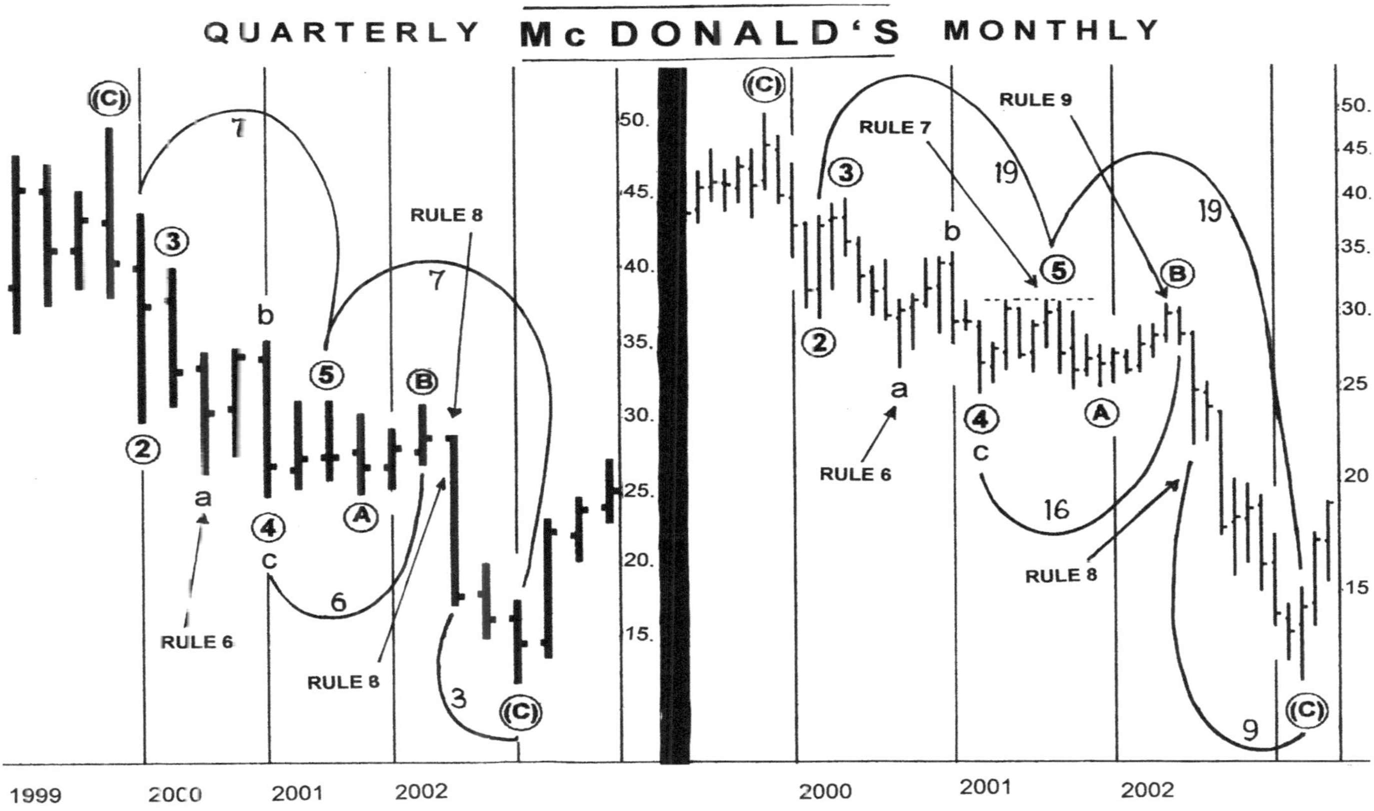

QUARTERLY McDONALD'S MONTHLY
RULE 6
RULE 8
RULE 8
RULE 7
RULE 9
RULE 6
RULE 8
1999
20C0
2001
2002
2000
2001
2002
50.
45.
40.
35.
30.
25.
20.
15.

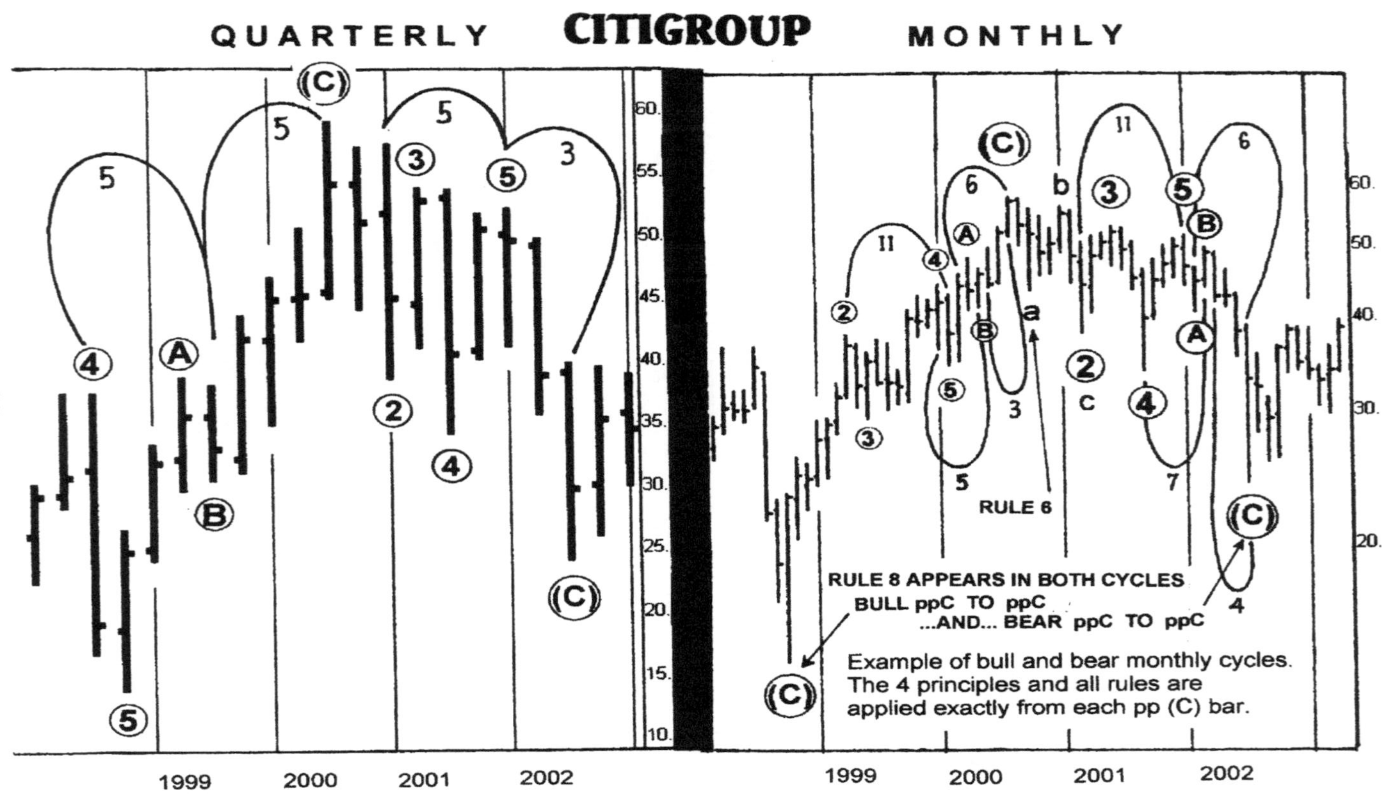

QUARTERLY
CITIGROUP
MONTHLY
RULE 6
RULE 8 APPEARS IN BOTH CYCLES
BULL ppC TO ppC
...AND... BEAR ppC TO ppC
Example of bull and bear monthly cycles.
The 4 principles and all rules are
applied exactly from each pp (C) bar.
1999
2000
2001
2002

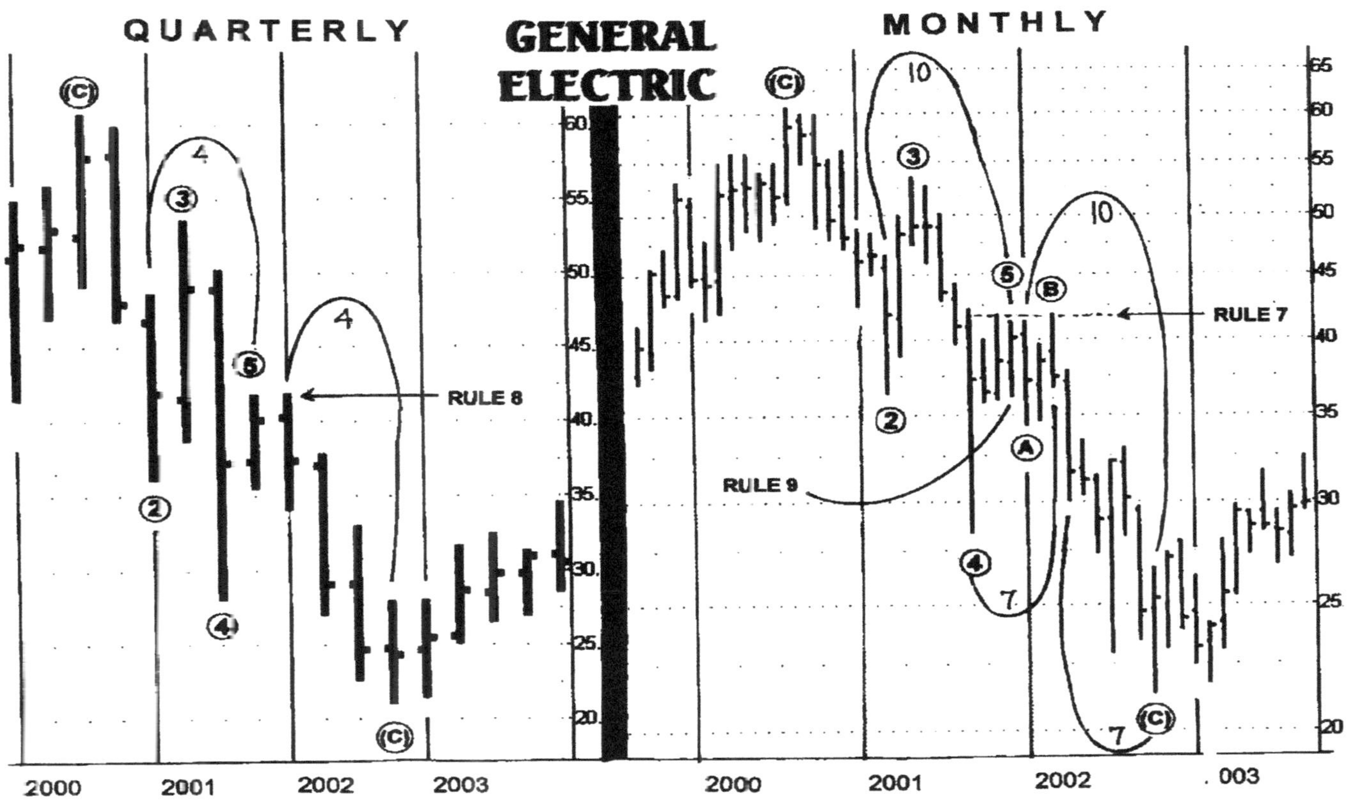
QUARTERLY
GENERAL ELECTRIC
MONTHLY
RULE 8
RULE 7
RULE 9
2000
2001
2002
2003
2000
2001
2002
. 003
65
60
55
50
45
40
35
30
25
20

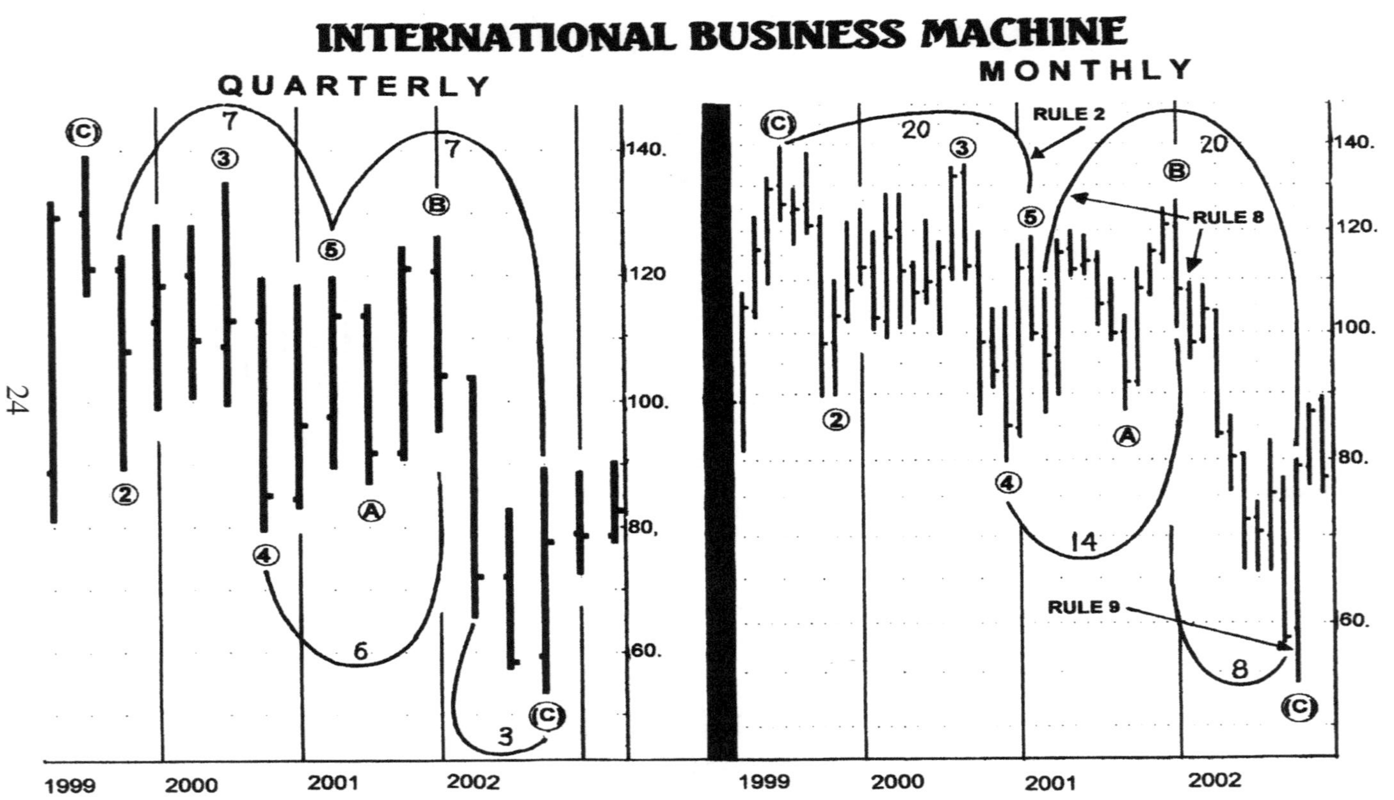
INTERNATIONAL BUSINESS MACHINE
QUARTERLY
MONTHLY
RULE 2
RULE 8
RULE 9
140.
120.
100.
80.
60.
1999
2000
2001
2002

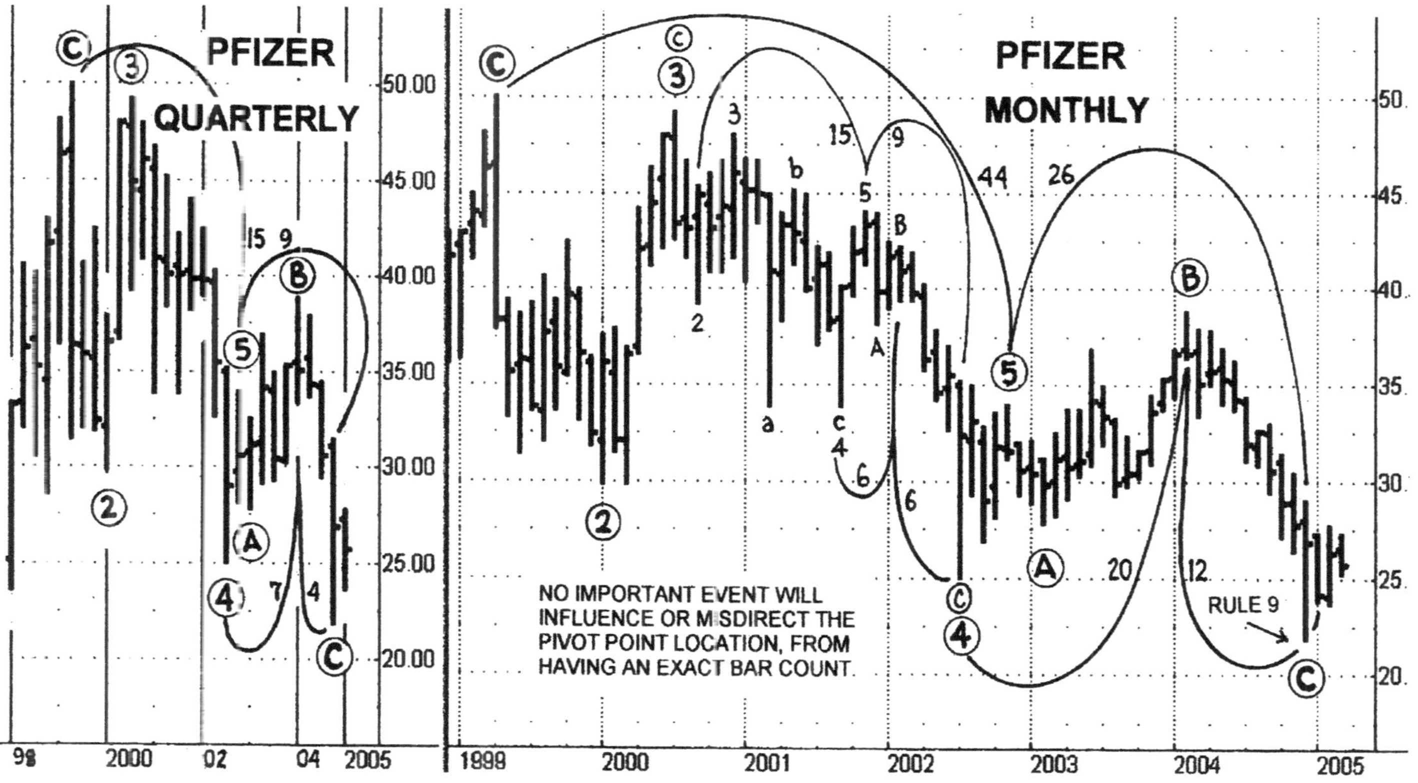
PFIZER
QUARTERLY
PFIZER
MONTHLY
NO IMPORTANT EVENT WILL
INFLUENCE OR MISDIRECT THE
PIVOT POINT LOCATION, FROM
HAVING AN EXACT BAR COUNT.
RULE 9

AT&T CORP.

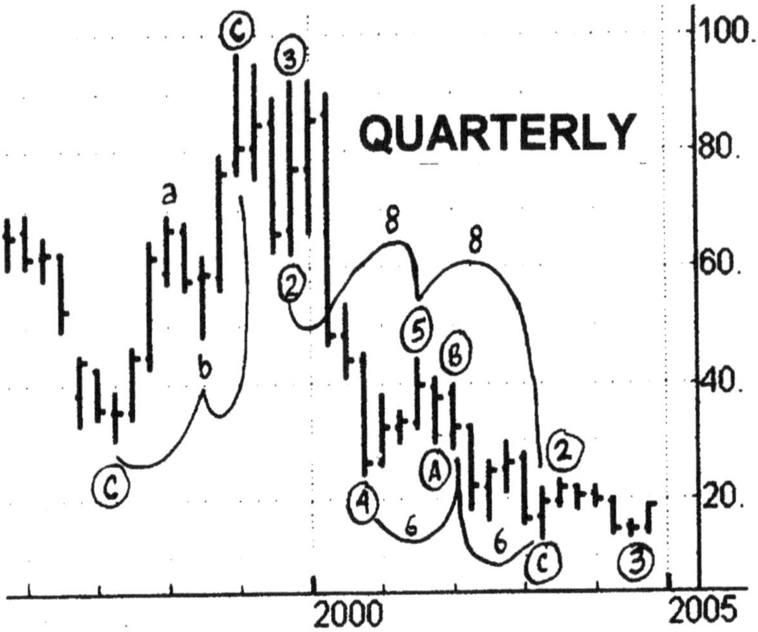

QUARTERLY

100.
80.
60.
40.
20.
2000
2005

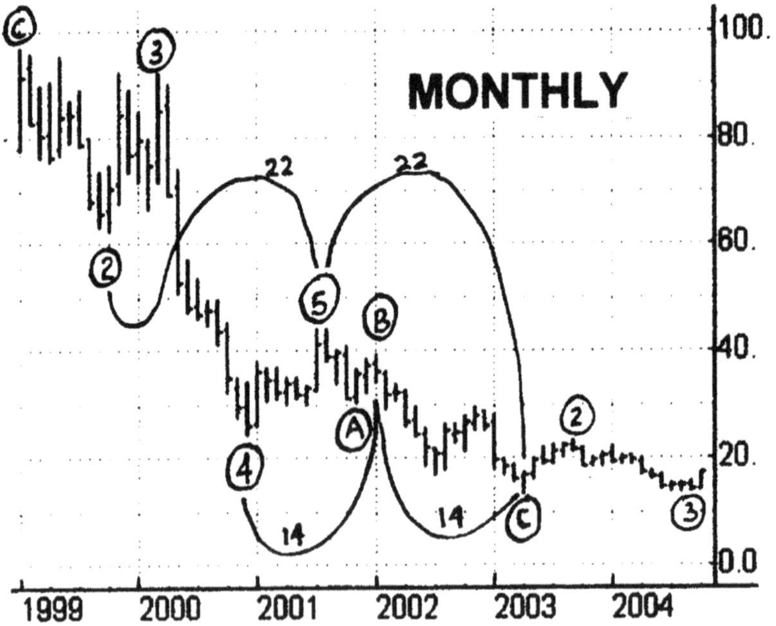

MONTHLY

100.
80.
60.
40.
20.
0.0
1999
2000
2001
2002
2003
2004

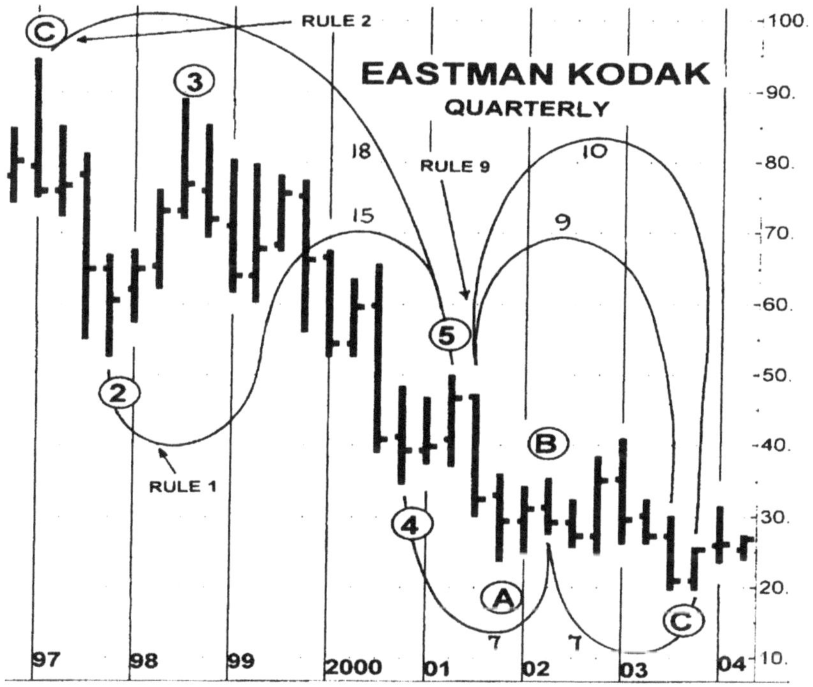

EASTMAN KODAK
QUARTERLY

RULE 2

RULE 9

RULE 1

97 98 99 2000 01 02 03 04

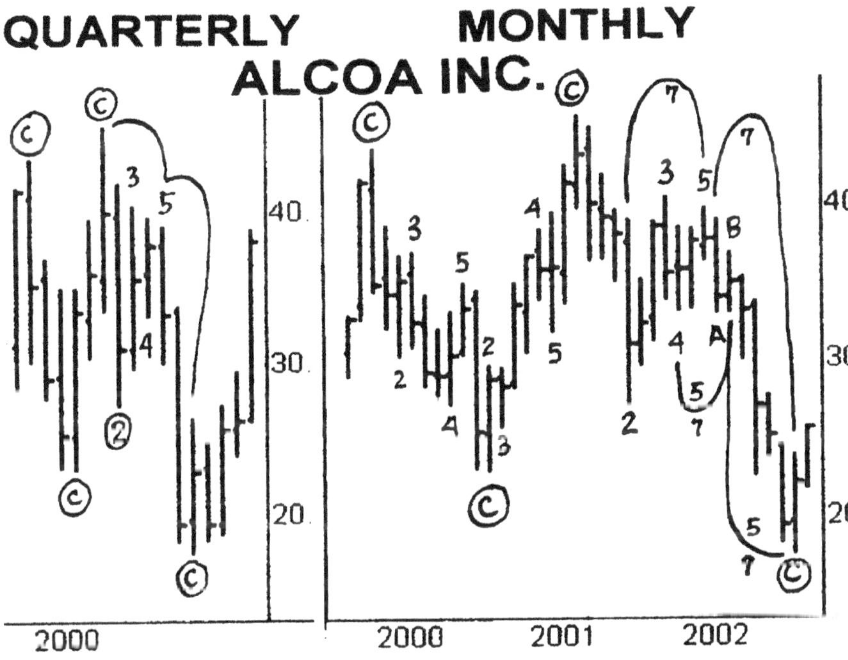

QUARTERLY MONTHLY
ALCOA INC.

2000

2000 2001 2002

SBC COMMUNICATIONS

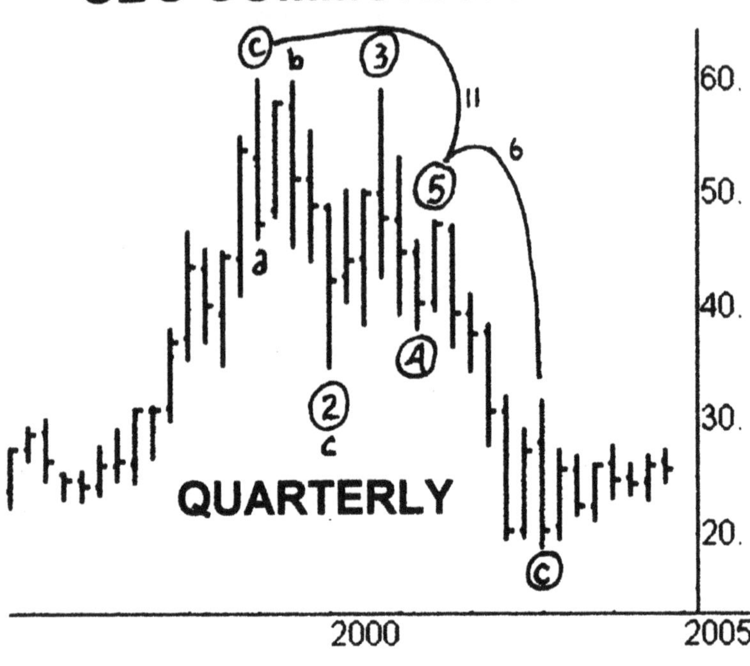

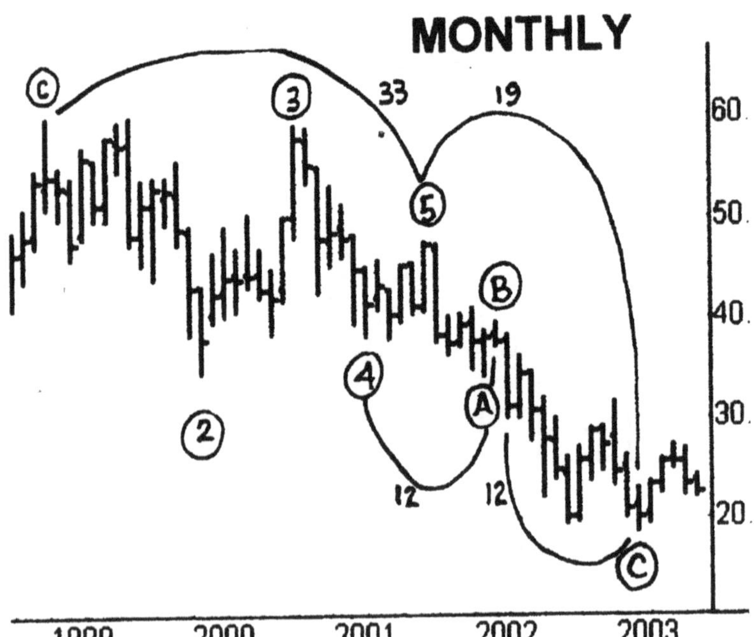

INTERNATIONAL PAPER

QUARTERLY **MONTHLY**

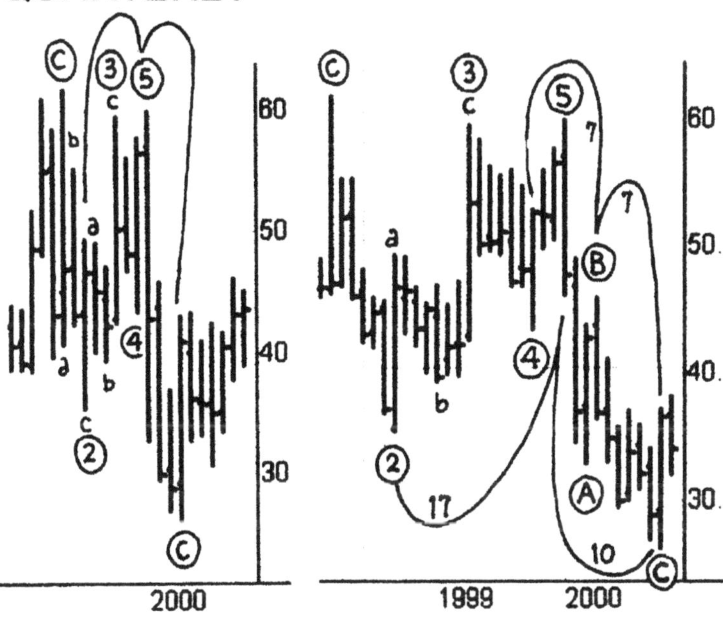

BOEING

QUARTERLY

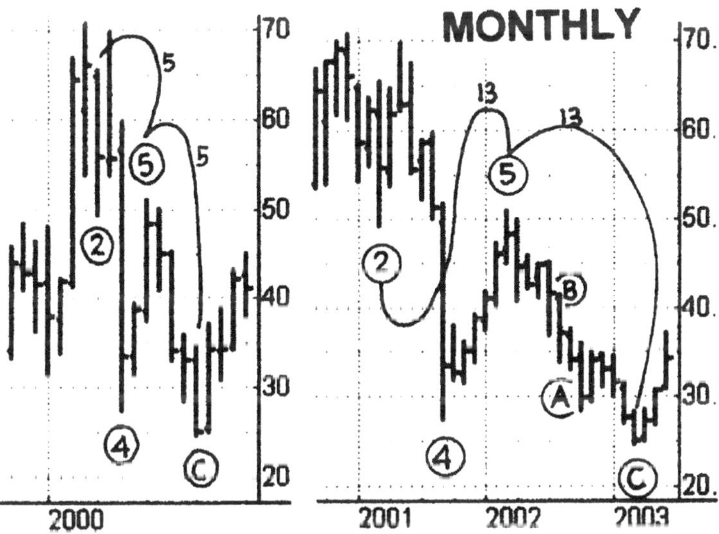

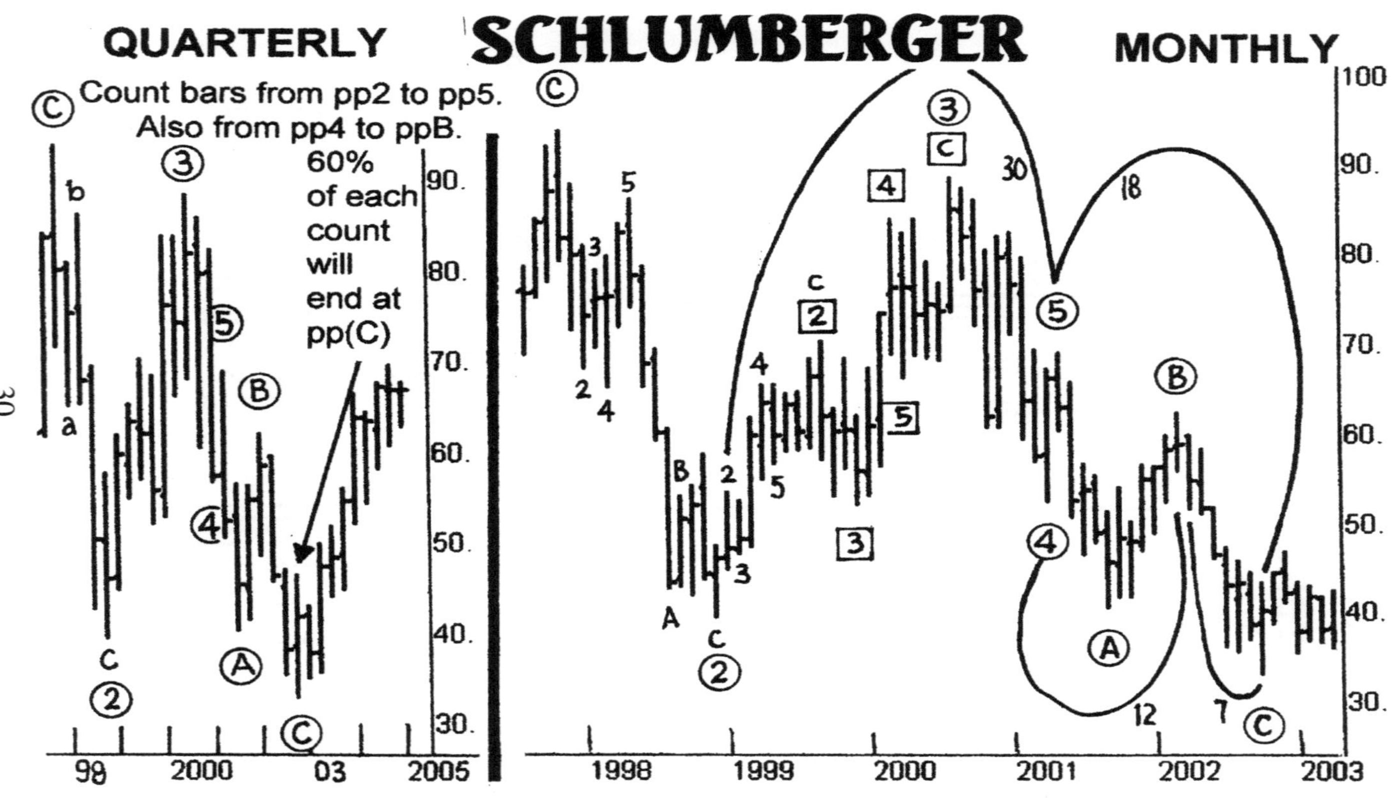
QUARTERLY
SCHLUMBERGER
MONTHLY
Count bars from pp2 to pp5.
Also from pp4 to ppB.
60%
of each
count
will
end at
pp(C)
99
2000
03
2005
1998
1999
2000
2001
2002
2003

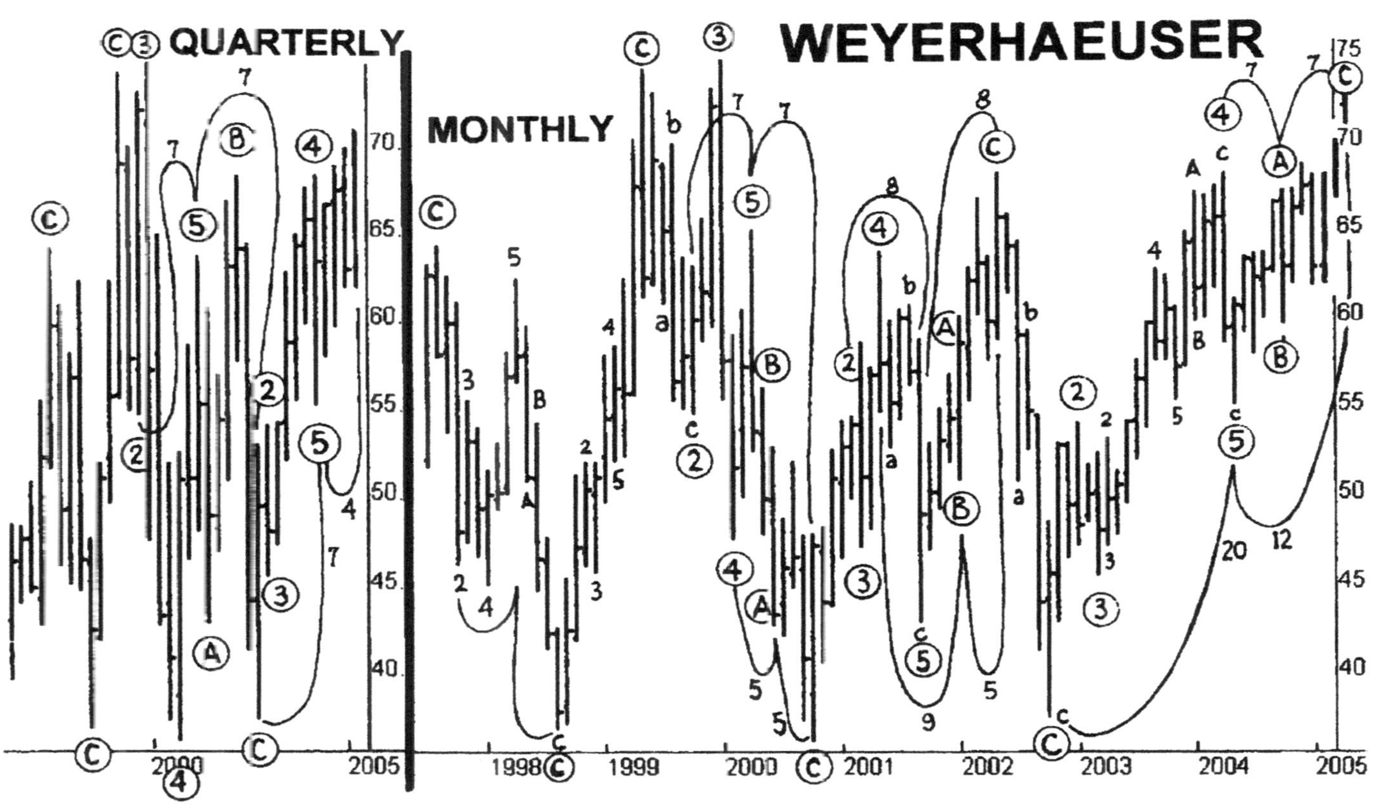
WEYERHAEUSER
QUARTERLY
MONTHLY

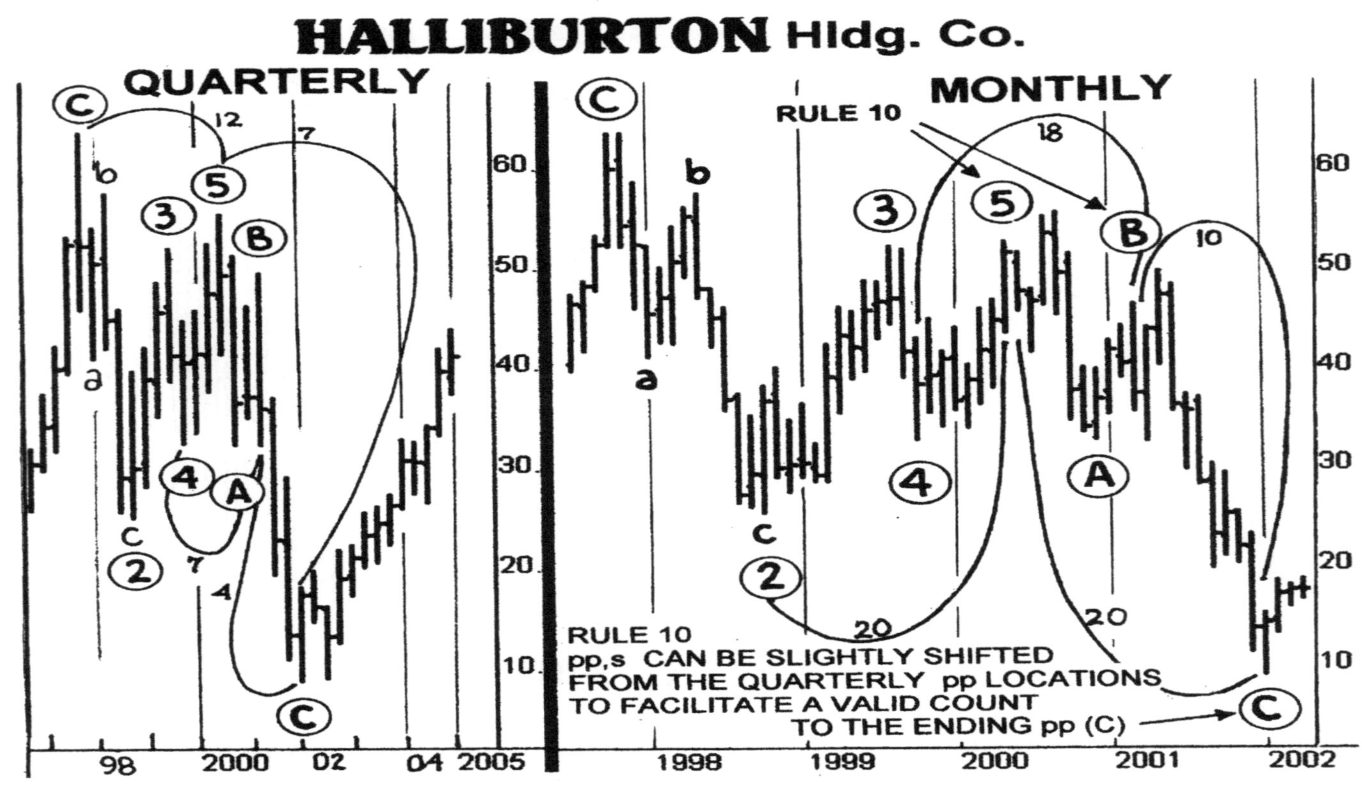
HALLIBURTON Hldg. Co.
QUARTERLY
MONTHLY
RULE 10
RULE 10
pp,s CAN BE SLIGHTLY SHIFTED
FROM THE QUARTERLY pp LOCATIONS
TO FACILITATE A VALID COUNT
TO THE ENDING pp (C)
60
50
40
30
20
10
98
2000
02
04
2005
1998
1999
2000
2001
2002

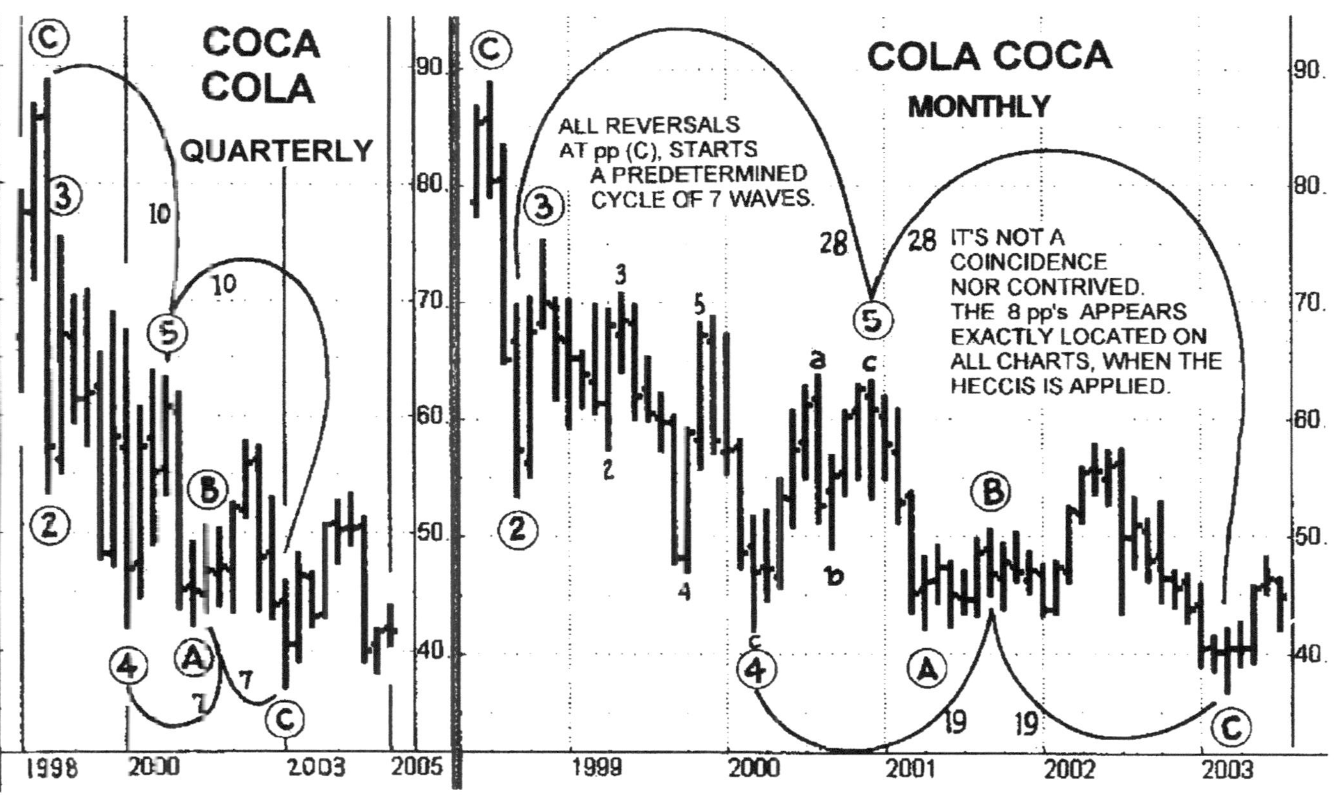
COCA COLA
QUARTERLY
COLA COCA
MONTHLY
ALL REVERSALS AT pp (C), STARTS A PREDETERMINED CYCLE OF 7 WAVES.
IT'S NOT A COINCIDENCE NOR CONTRIVED. THE 8 pp's APPEARS EXACTLY LOCATED ON ALL CHARTS, WHEN THE HECCIS IS APPLIED.
1998
2000
2003
2005
1999
2001
2002
90
80
70
60
50
40
10
28
19
7

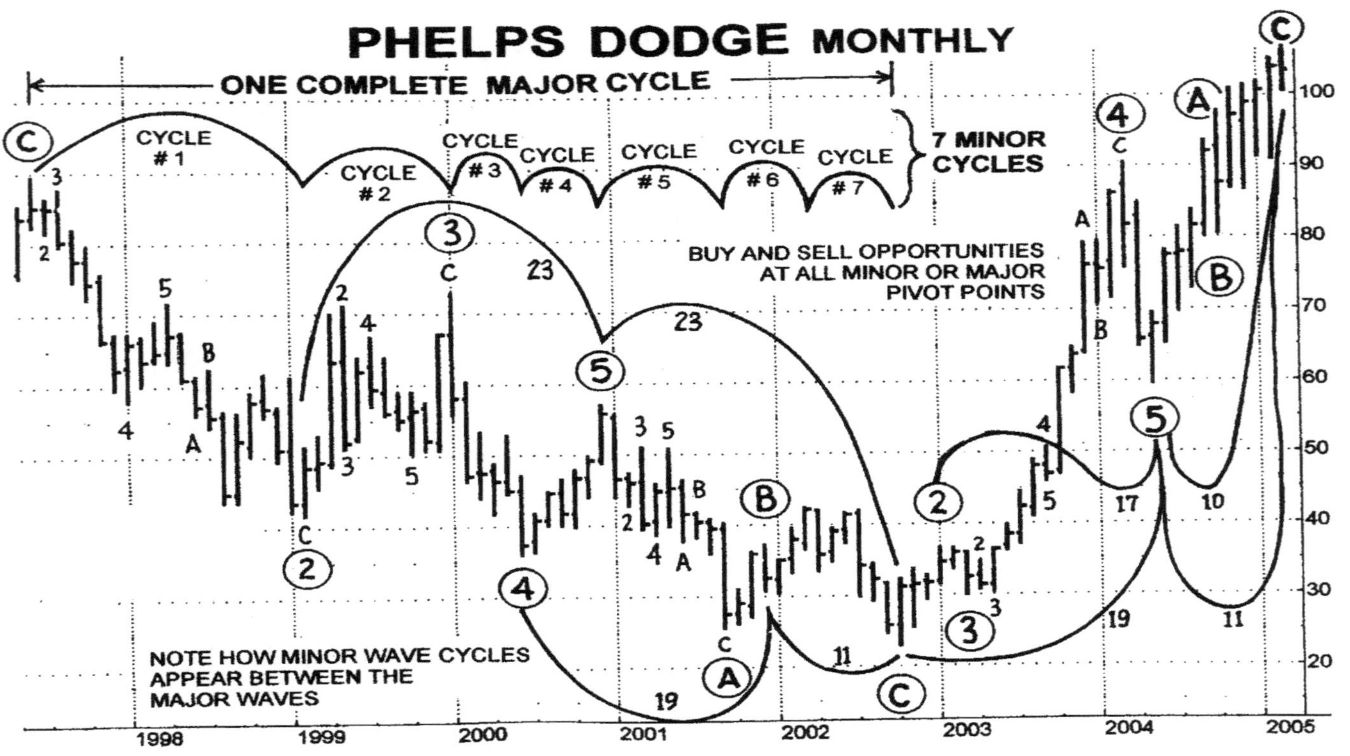

PHELPS DODGE MONTHLY
ONE COMPLETE MAJOR CYCLE
CYCLE #1
CYCLE #2
CYCLE #3
CYCLE #4
CYCLE #5
CYCLE #6
CYCLE #7
7 MINOR CYCLES
BUY AND SELL OPPORTUNITIES AT ALL MINOR OR MAJOR PIVOT POINTS
NOTE HOW MINOR WAVE CYCLES APPEAR BETWEEN THE MAJOR WAVES
1998
1999
2000
2001
2002
2003
2004
2005
100
90
80
70
60
50
40
30
20

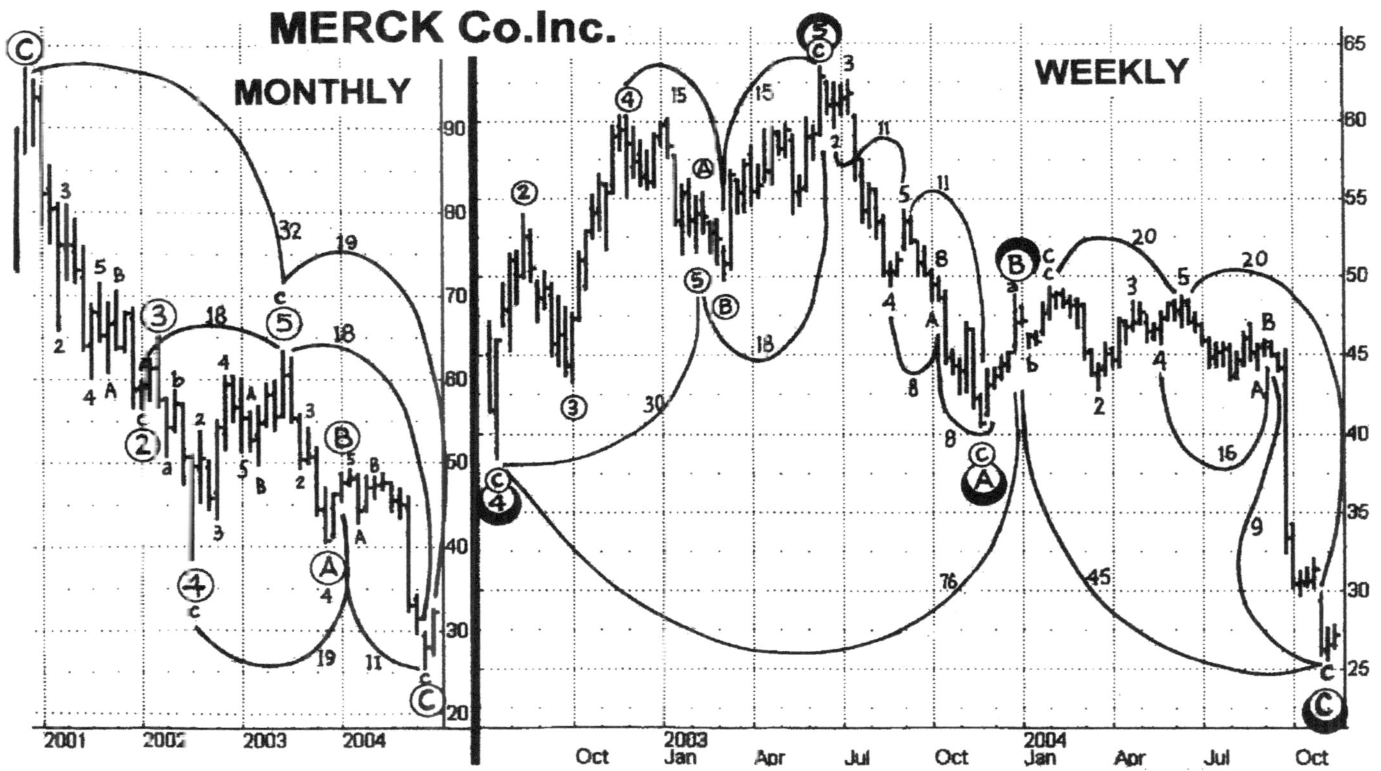
MERCK Co.Inc.
MONTHLY
WEEKLY

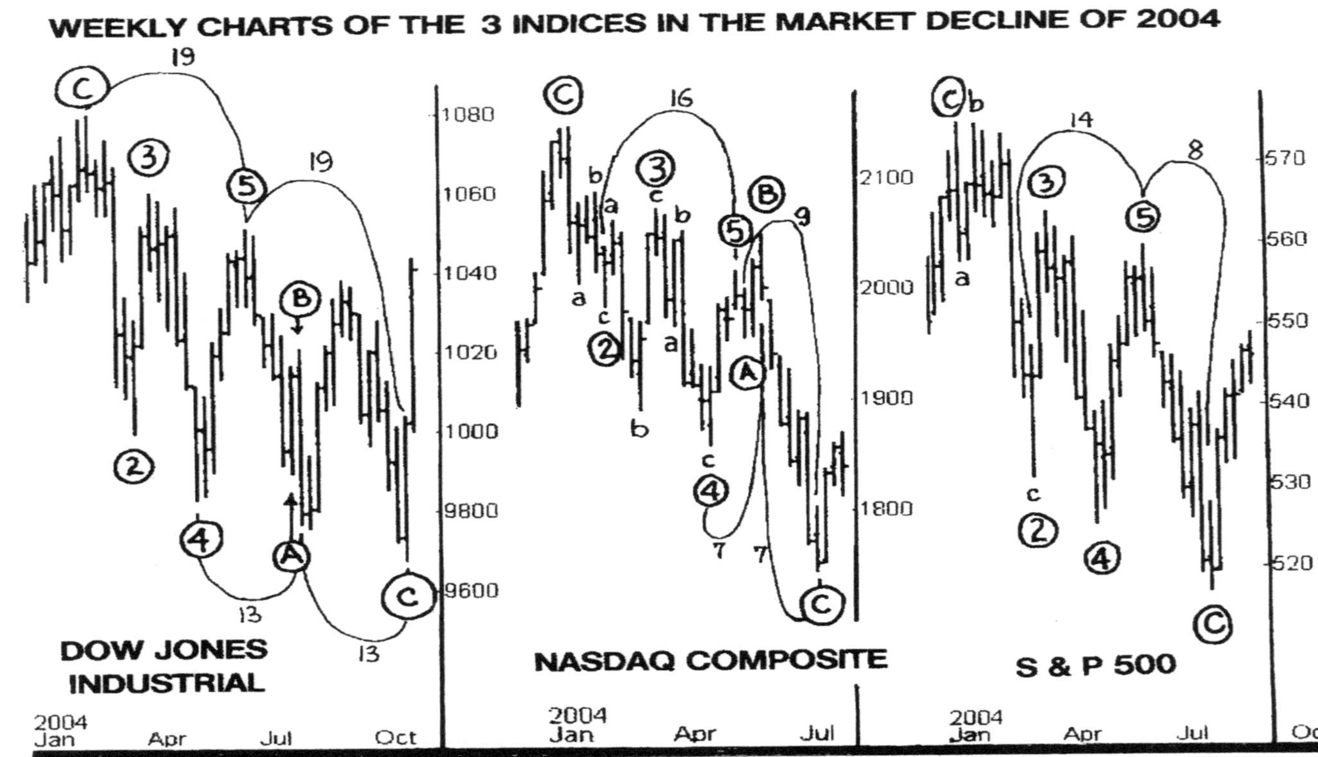

WEEKLY CHARTS OF THE 3 INDICES IN THE MARKET DECLINE OF 2004
DOW JONES INDUSTRIAL
NASDAQ COMPOSITE
S & P 500
1080
1060
1040
1020
1000
9800
9600
2100
2000
1900
1800
570
560
550
540
530
520
2004 Jan
Apr
Jul
Oct

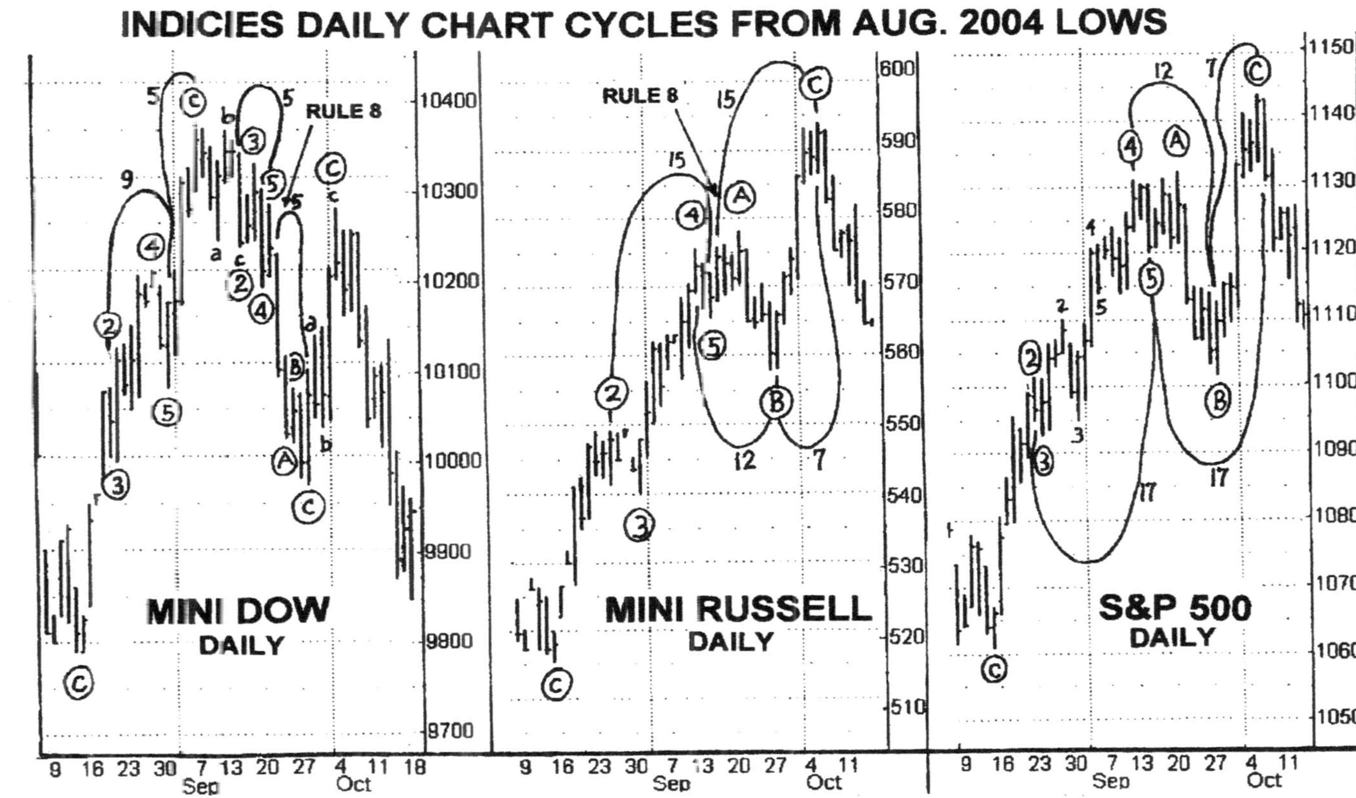
INDICIES DAILY CHART CYCLES FROM AUG. 2004 LOWS
MINI DOW
DAILY
MINI RUSSELL
DAILY
S&P 500
DAILY
RULE 8
RULE 8
Sep
Oct
Sep
Oct
Sep
Oct

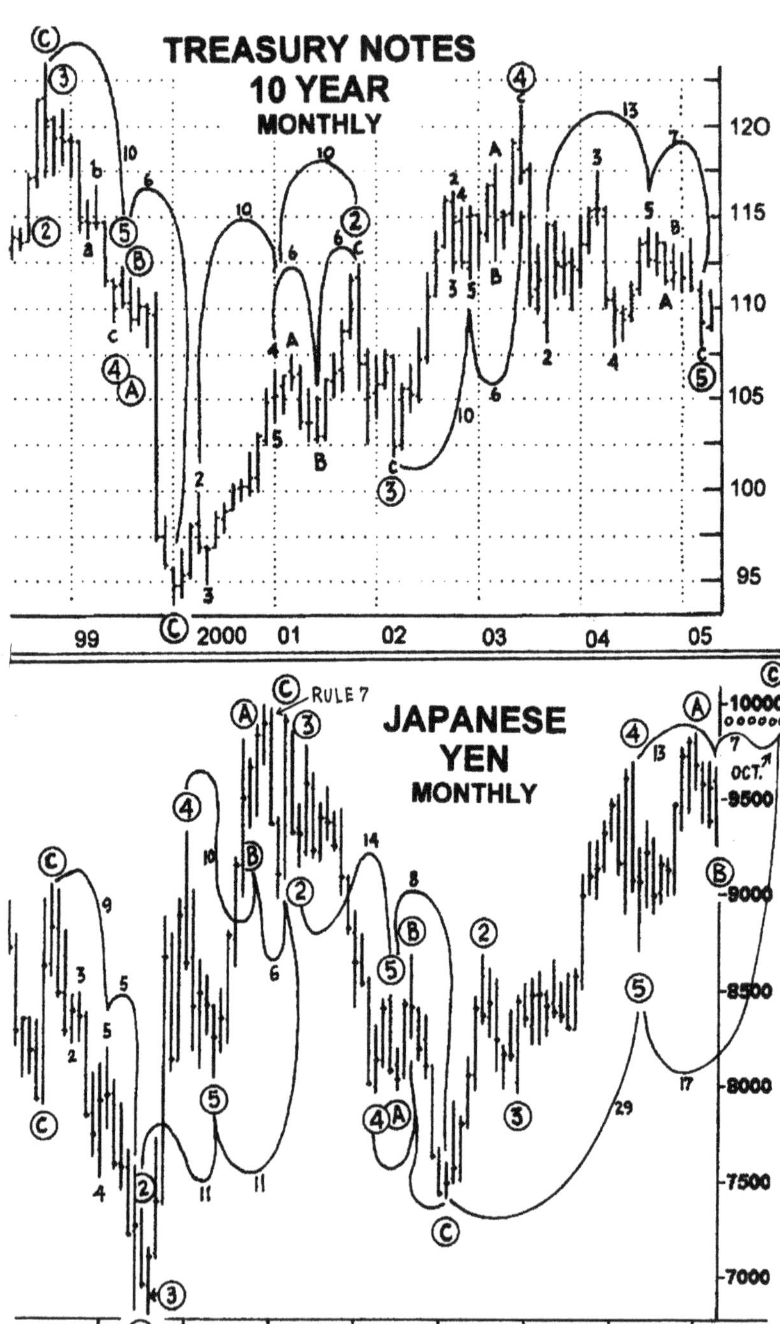

Created with SuperCharts by Omega Research © 1997

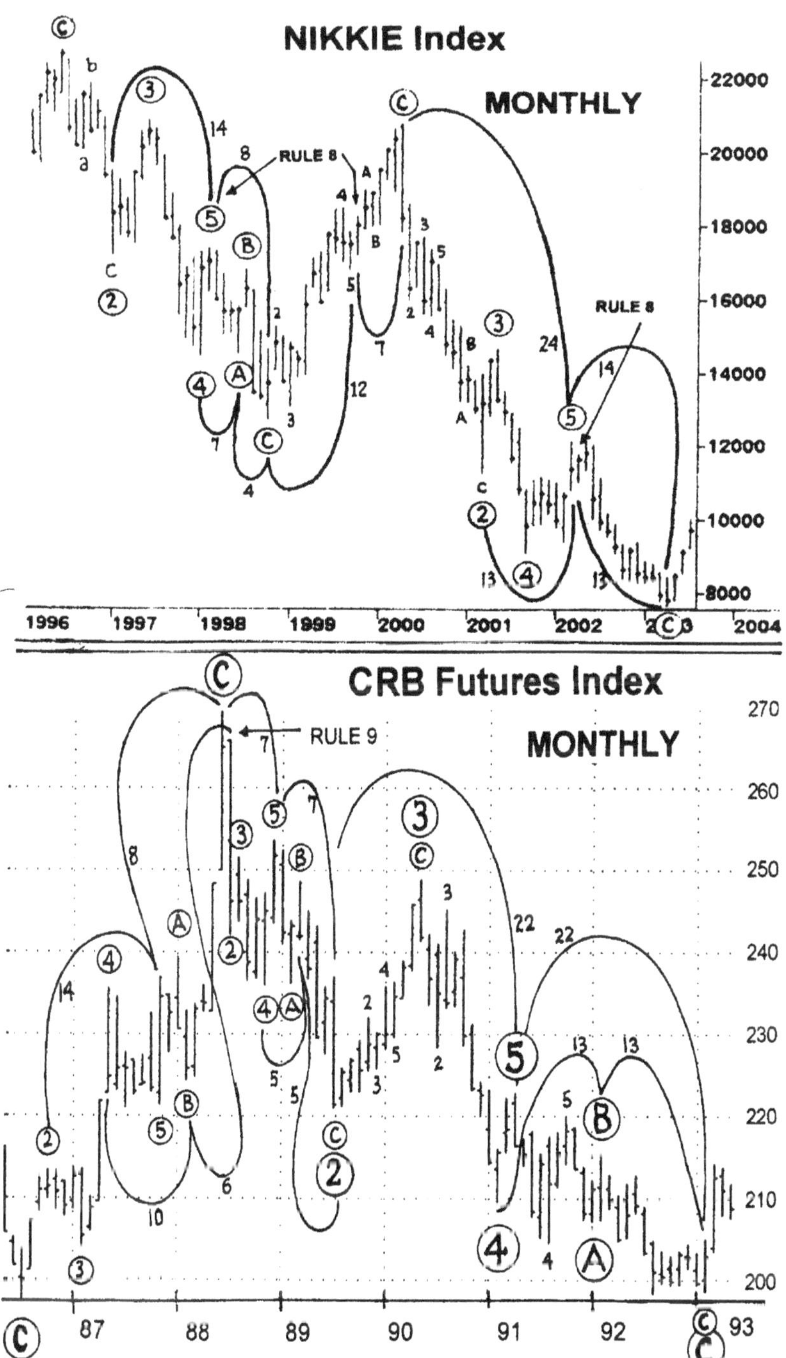
NIKKIE Index
MONTHLY
RULE 8
RULE 8
22000
20000
18000
16000
14000
12000
10000
8000
1996
1997
1998
1999
2000
2001
2002
2004
CRB Futures Index
MONTHLY
RULE 9
270
260
250
240
230
220
210
200
87
88
89
90
91
92
93

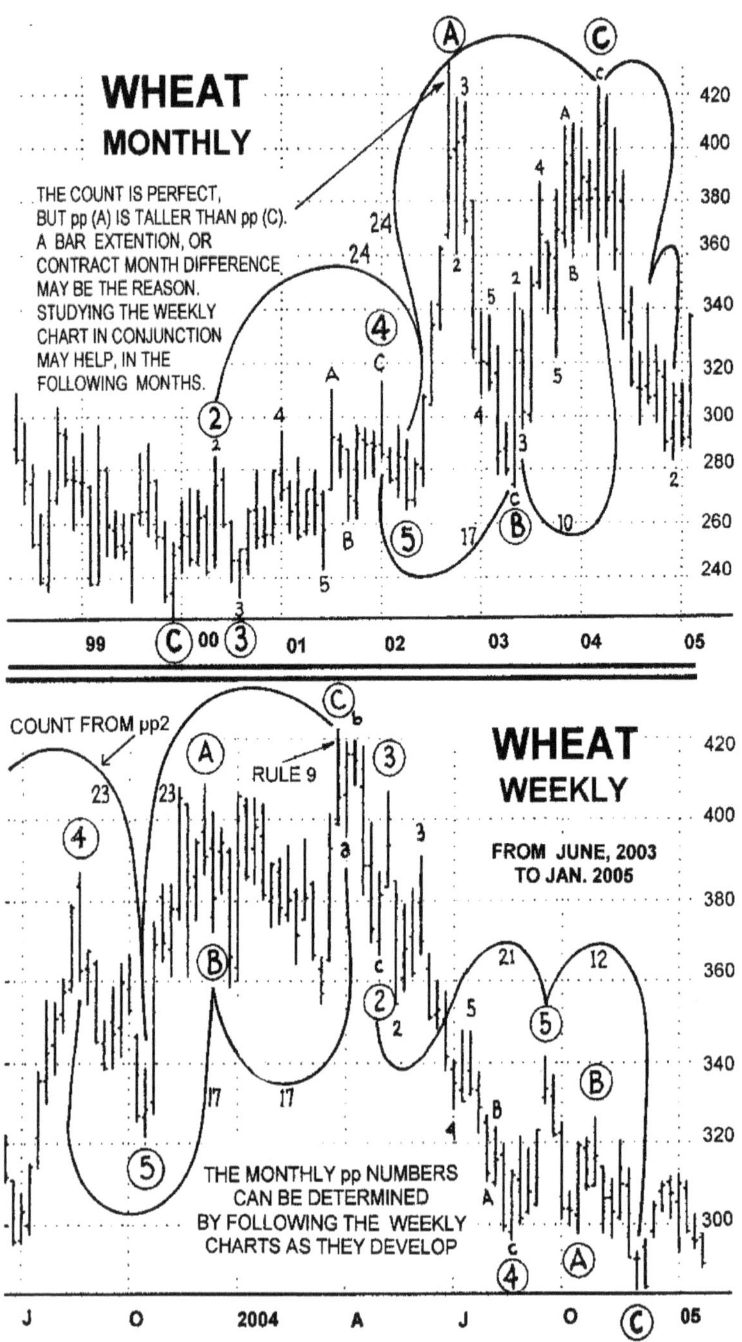
WHEAT
MONTHLY
THE COUNT IS PERFECT,
BUT pp (A) IS TALLER THAN pp (C).
A BAR EXTENTION, OR
CONTRACT MONTH DIFFERENCE
MAY BE THE REASON.
STUDYING THE WEEKLY
CHART IN CONJUNCTION
MAY HELP, IN THE
FOLLOWING MONTHS.
99
00
01
02
03
04
05
420
400
380
360
340
320
300
280
260
240
COUNT FROM pp2
RULE 9
WHEAT
WEEKLY
FROM JUNE, 2003
TO JAN. 2005
THE MONTHLY pp NUMBERS
CAN BE DETERMINED
BY FOLLOWING THE WEEKLY
CHARTS AS THEY DEVELOP
J
O
2004
A
J
O
05

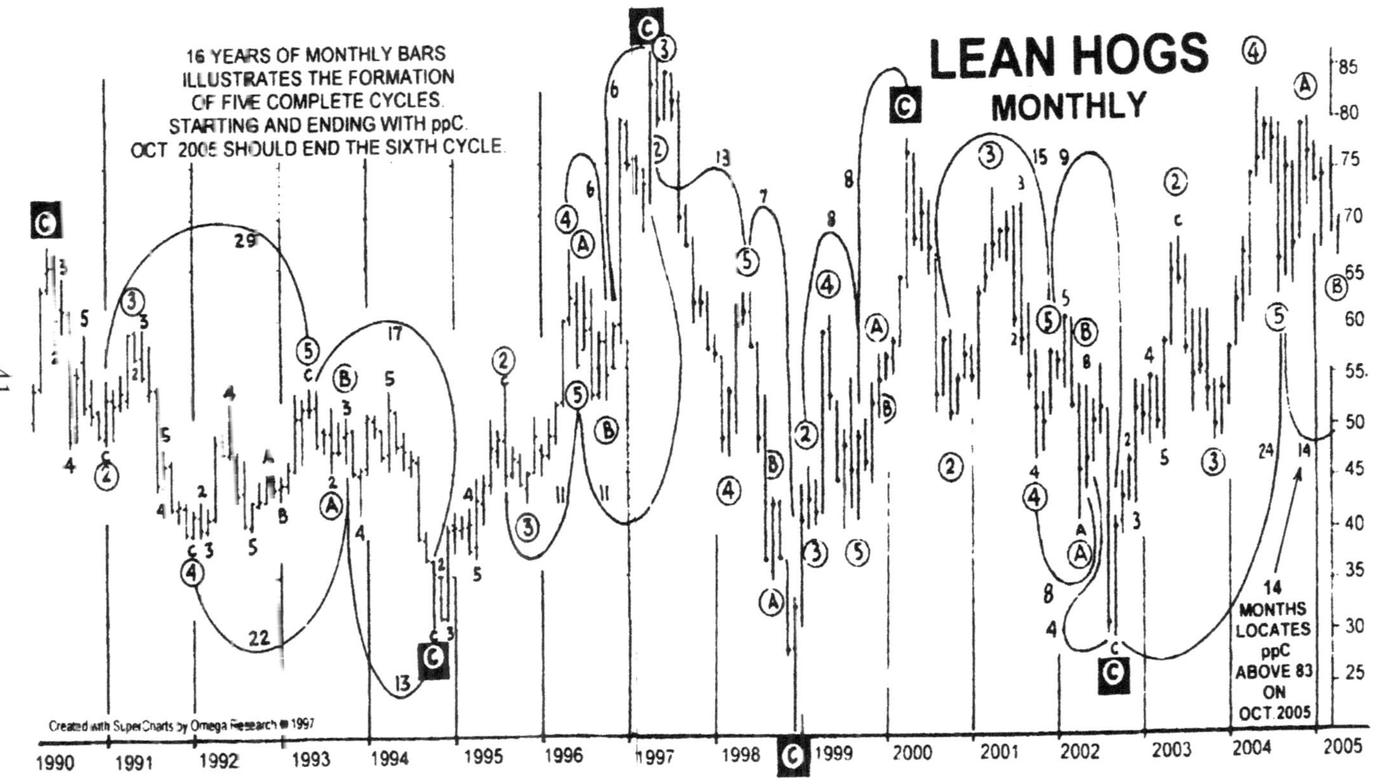
LEAN HOGS
MONTHLY
16 YEARS OF MONTHLY BARS
ILLUSTRATES THE FORMATION
OF FIVE COMPLETE CYCLES.
STARTING AND ENDING WITH ppC.
OCT 2005 SHOULD END THE SIXTH CYCLE.
14
MONTHS
LOCATES
ppC
ABOVE 83
ON
OCT 2005
1990 1991 1992 1993 1994 1995 1996 1997 1998 1999 2000 2001 2002 2003 2004 2005
85 80 75 70 65 60 55 50 45 40 35 30 25
Created with SuperCharts by Omega Research © 1997

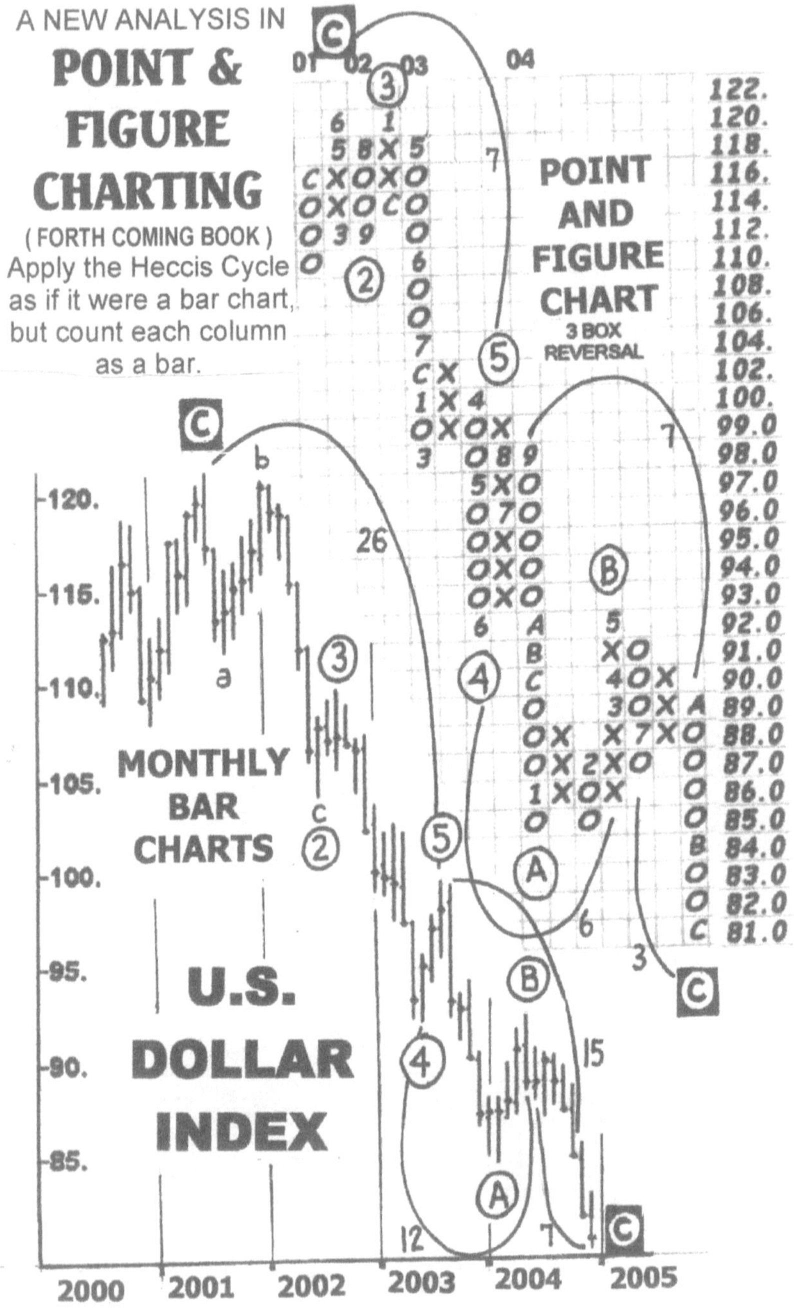
A NEW ANALYSIS IN
POINT &
FIGURE
CHARTING
(FORTH COMING BOOK)
Apply the Heccis Cycle as if it were a bar chart, but count each column as a bar.
POINT AND FIGURE CHART
3 BOX REVERSAL
01 02 03 04
122. 120. 118. 116. 114. 112. 110. 108. 106. 104. 102. 100. 99.0 98.0 97.0 96.0 95.0 94.0 93.0 92.0 91.0 90.0 89.0 88.0 87.0 86.0 85.0 84.0 83.0 82.0 81.0
MONTHLY BAR CHARTS
U.S. DOLLAR INDEX
120. 115. 110. 105. 100. 95. 90. 85.
2000 2001 2002 2003 2004 2005
26
15
12

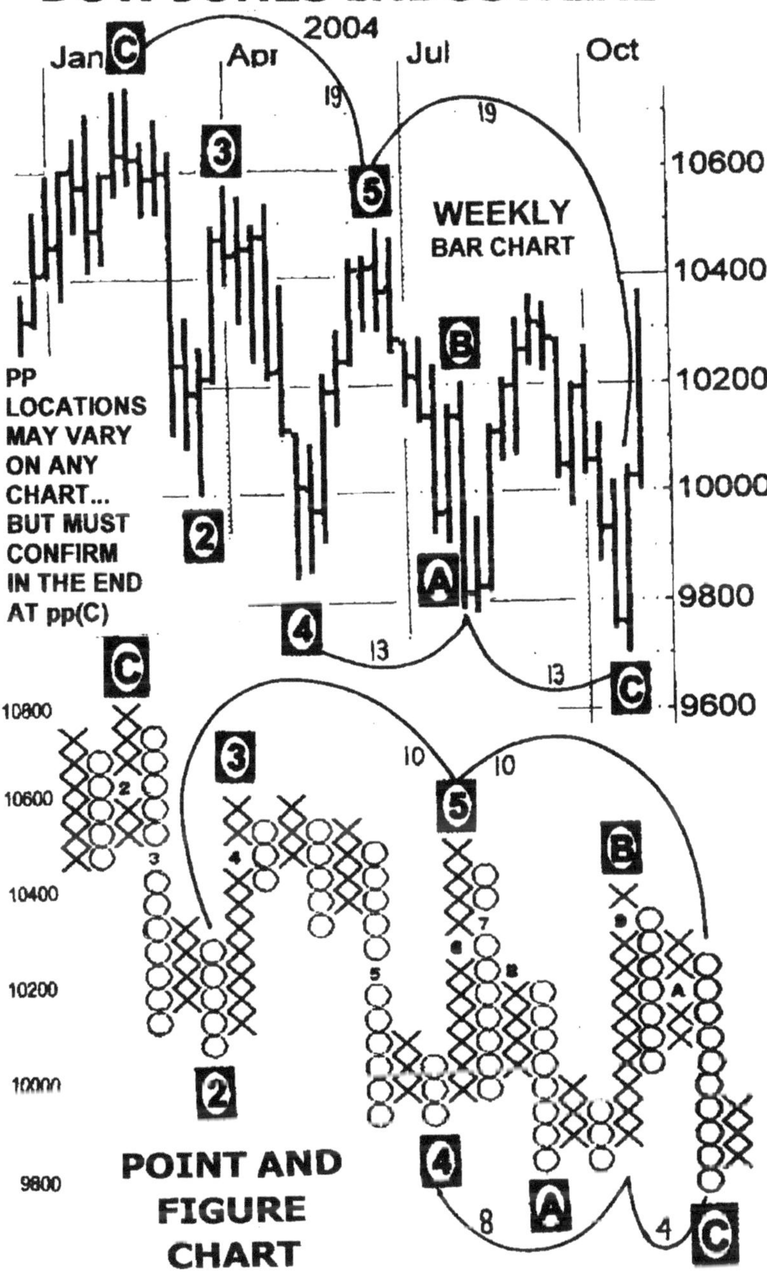

(c) StockCharts.com

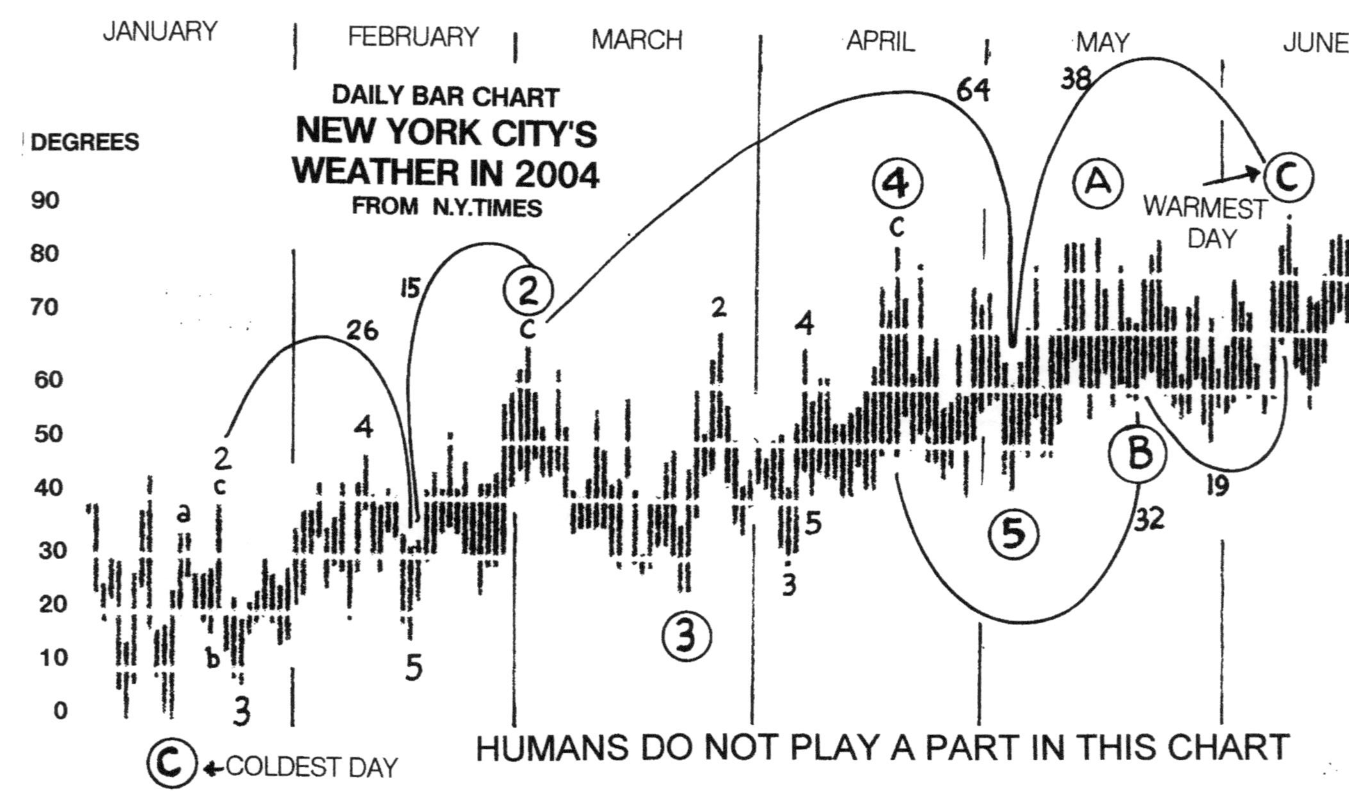
DAILY BAR CHART
NEW YORK CITY'S
WEATHER IN 2004
FROM N.Y.TIMES
DEGREES
90
80
70
60
50
40
30
20
10
0
JANUARY
FEBRUARY
MARCH
APRIL
MAY
JUNE
a
b
c
2
3
26
4
15
5
2
c
2
3
4
5
3
4
c
64
5
38
A
B
32
19
C
WARMEST DAY
C
←COLDEST DAY
HUMANS DO NOT PLAY A PART IN THIS CHART

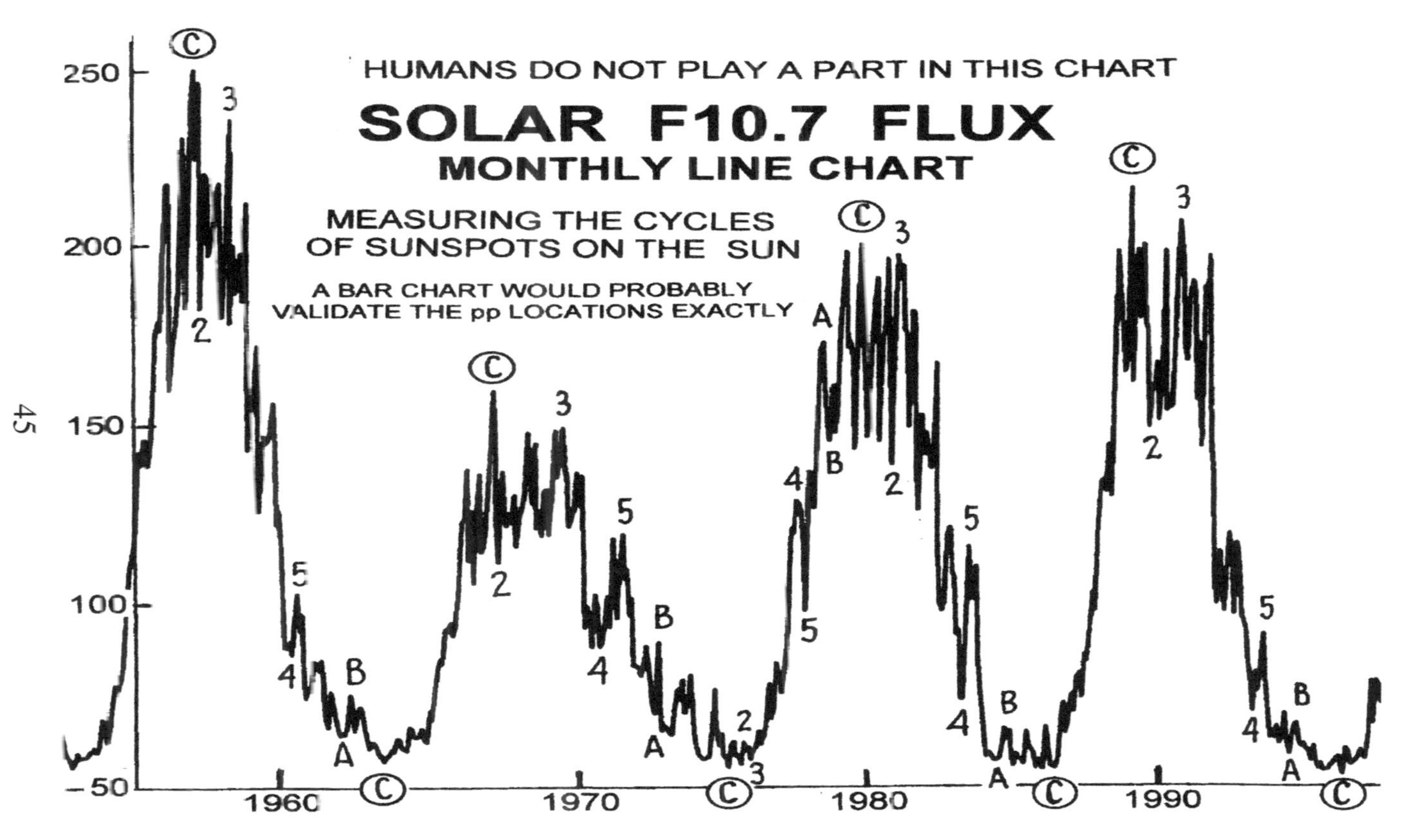
HUMANS DO NOT PLAY A PART IN THIS CHART
SOLAR F10.7 FLUX
MONTHLY LINE CHART
MEASURING THE CYCLES
OF SUNSPOTS ON THE SUN
A BAR CHART WOULD PROBABLY
VALIDATE THE pp LOCATIONS EXACTLY
250
200
150
100
50
1960
1970
1980
1990

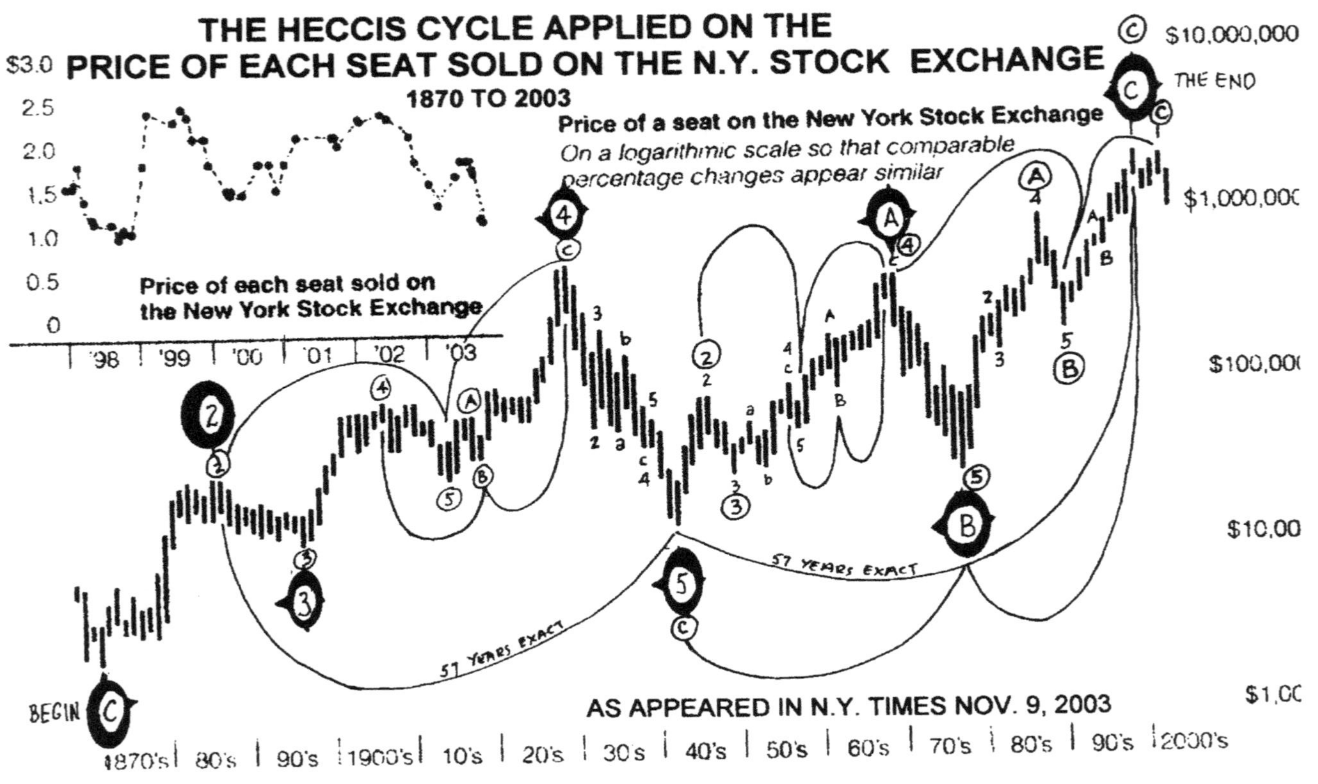
THE HECCIS CYCLE APPLIED ON THE
PRICE OF EACH SEAT SOLD ON THE N.Y. STOCK EXCHANGE
1870 TO 2003
Price of a seat on the New York Stock Exchange
On a logarithmic scale so that comparable percentage changes appear similar
Price of each seat sold on the New York Stock Exchange
$3.0
2.5
2.0
1.5
1.0
0.5
0
'98
'99
'00
'01
'02
'03
$10,000,000
$1,000,000
$100,000
$10,000
$1,000
THE END
BEGIN
57 YEARS EXACT
57 YEARS EXACT
AS APPEARED IN N.Y. TIMES NOV. 9, 2003
1870's
80's
90's
1900's
10's
20's
30's
40's
50's
60's
70's
80's
90's
2000's

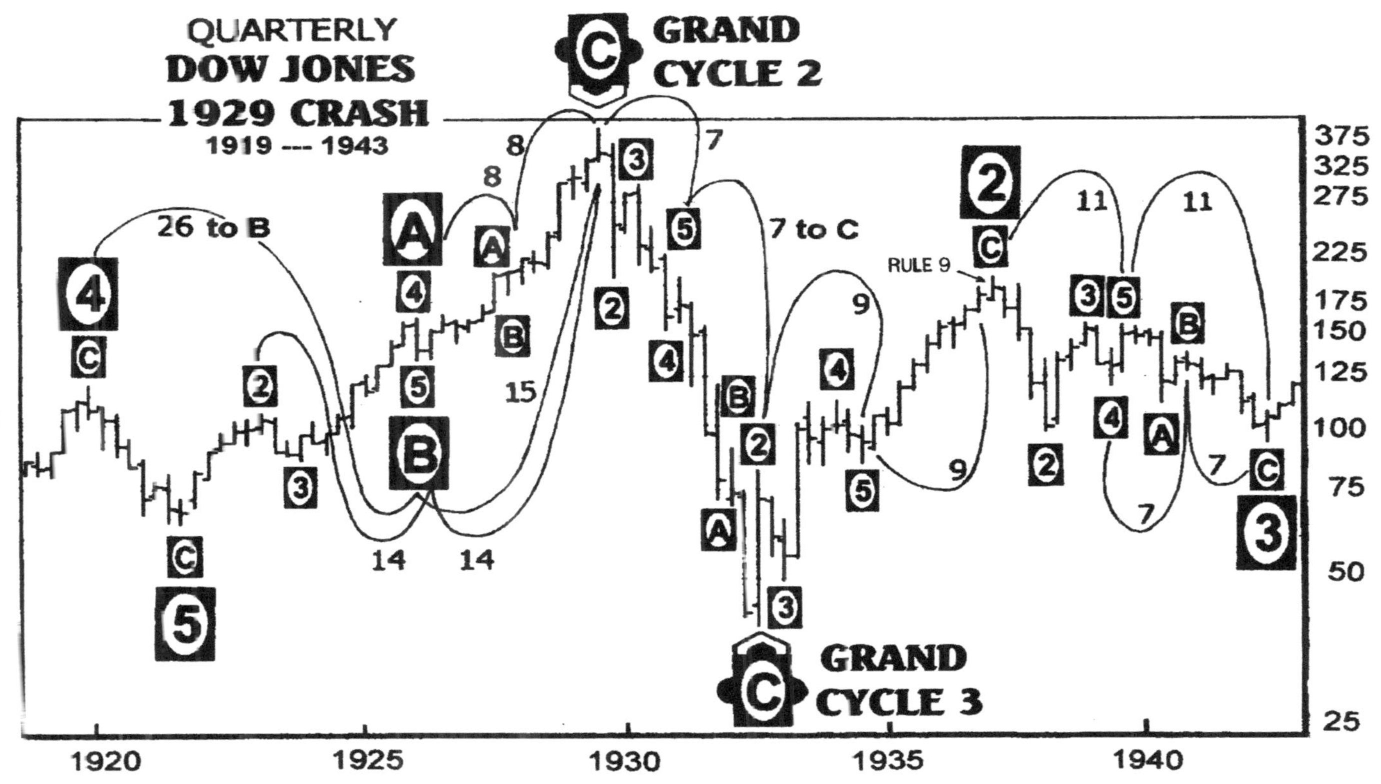
QUARTERLY
DOW JONES
1929 CRASH
1919 --- 1943
GRAND
CYCLE 2
GRAND
CYCLE 3
26 to B
7 to C
RULE 9
375
325
275
225
175
150
125
100
75
50
25
1920
1925
1930
1935
1940

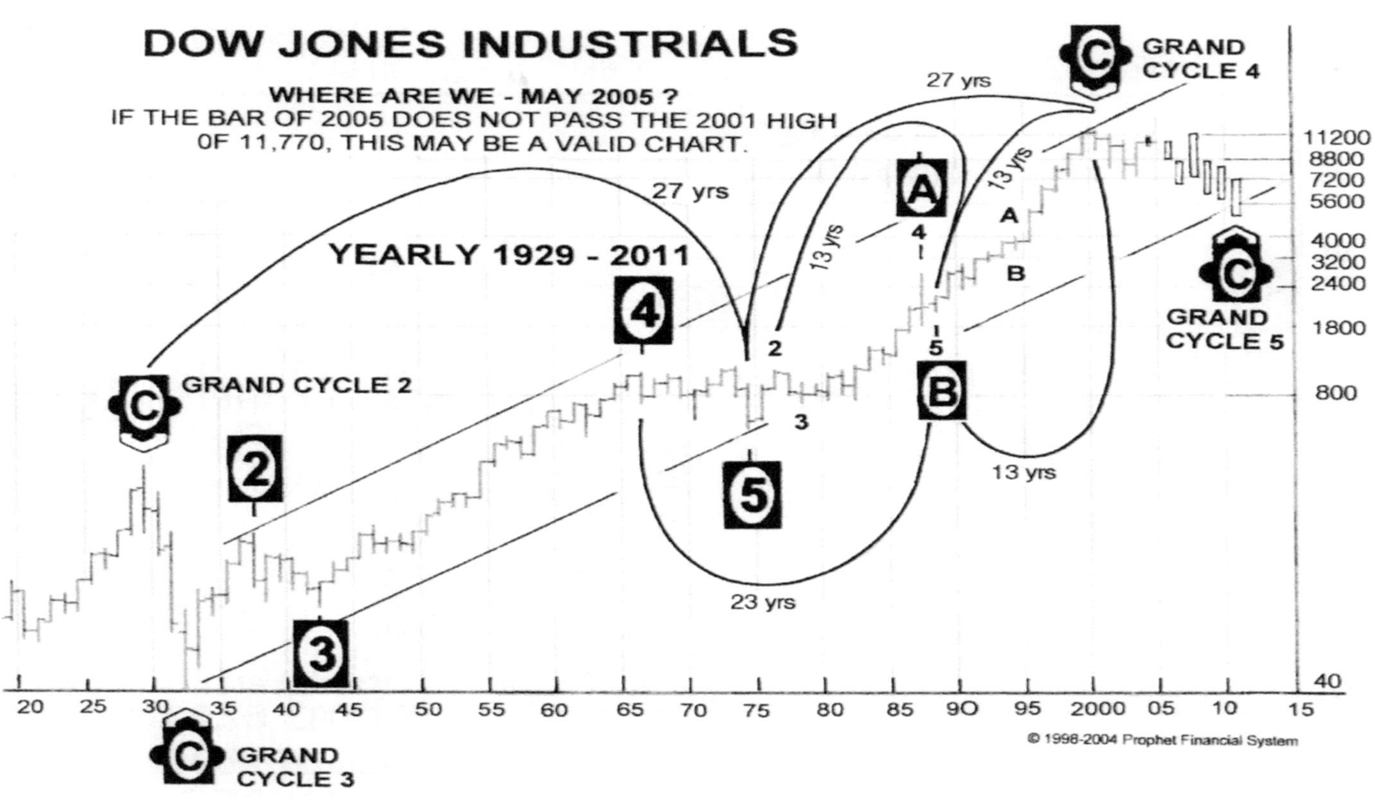

DOW JONES INDUSTRIALS
WHERE ARE WE - MAY 2005 ?
IF THE BAR OF 2005 DOES NOT PASS THE 2001 HIGH
OF 11,770, THIS MAY BE A VALID CHART.
YEARLY 1929 - 2011
GRAND CYCLE 2
GRAND CYCLE 3
GRAND CYCLE 4
GRAND CYCLE 5
27 yrs
27 yrs
13 yrs
13 yrs
13 yrs
23 yrs
2
3
4
5
A
B
11200
8800
7200
5600
4000
3200
2400
1800
800
40
20 25 30 35 40 45 50 55 60 65 70 75 80 85 90 95 2000 05 10 15
© 1998-2004 Prophet Financial System

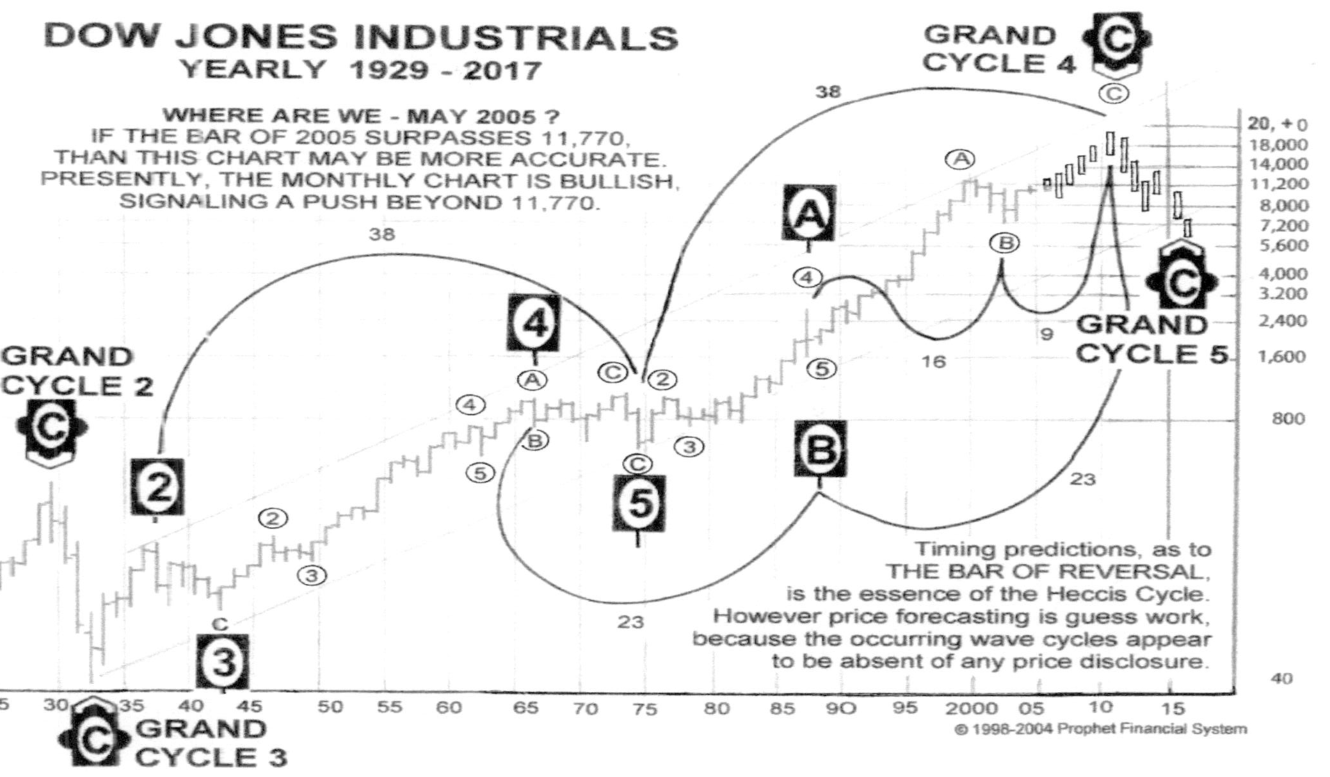
DOW JONES INDUSTRIALS
YEARLY 1929 - 2017
WHERE ARE WE - MAY 2005 ?
IF THE BAR OF 2005 SURPASSES 11,770,
THAN THIS CHART MAY BE MORE ACCURATE.
PRESENTLY, THE MONTHLY CHART IS BULLISH,
SIGNALING A PUSH BEYOND 11,770.
GRAND CYCLE 2
GRAND CYCLE 3
GRAND CYCLE 4
GRAND CYCLE 5
38
38
23
23
16
9
Timing predictions, as to
THE BAR OF REVERSAL,
is the essence of the Heccis Cycle.
However price forecasting is guess work,
because the occurring wave cycles appear
to be absent of any price disclosure.
25 30 35 40 45 50 55 60 65 70 75 80 85 90 95 2000 05 10 15
20, +0 18,000 14,000 11,200 8,000 7,200 5,600 4,000 3,200 2,400 1,600 800 40
© 1998-2004 Prophet Financial System

In my judgment, the bar counting method of the Heccis Cycle is a vast improvement over any wave principals, in practice by today's technical analysis's. If you agree, don't assume as other wave advocates that it is complete or final. I suggest further studies into the ordinary looking bar charts for other hidden information that may be there to unfold.

I hope after your careful analysis of the charts you have found the Heccis Cycle a convincing tool for your investment objectives. It has pleased me to disclose this discovery and to start three more books this coming year.
The titles;
COUNTING THE P&F COLUMNS
IN THE HECCIS CYCLE
The easy new way to market timing

COUNTING THE HOURS
IN THE HECCIS CYCLE
The easy way for Swing Traders

COUNTING THE MINUTES
IN THE HECCIS CYCLE
The easy way to Day Trading

Hector Cisneros can be reached at....heccis.com

www.ingramcontent.com/pod-product-compliance
Ingram Content Group UK Ltd.
Pitfield, Milton Keynes, MK11 3LW, UK
UKHW041844190726
13854UKWH00002B/707

9 781412 057318